"In touchingly plain language, Chris Mercogliano tells about twenty-five years of unfolding trust; how kids learn without anyone making sure; how a free school has become the pretext for community; and how adults who care are able, by shedding their roles, to open unexpected spaces for friendship and new growth. More convincing than any book I have had the privilege to read, this one proves that learning by children ought, once and for all, to be institutionally disembedded."

—**Ivan Illich,** *author of* Deschooling Society

"Chris Mercogliano's story about how non-professional adults and impoverished children learn together—not just inside the walls of Albany's Free School, but within the entire community—proves dramatically that there are more important and nurturing outcomes for students than higher test scores. Mercogliano is able to make us feel the urgency of his message by thoughtfully describing how the children he works with have changed his life and his ideas about what school can be.

"This is a brave and invigorating account of what is possible for ordinary people to accomplish within the cracks and holes of our increasingly monolithic and standardized education system."

—**Patrick Farenga,** *President of John Holt Associates*

"This is a genuinely wonderful book. Most importantly, it demonstrates how community can transcend the elitism, classism and atomism to which so much of the alternative education movement has fallen prey. I am consistently inspired by the dignity and vision of Chris and the Albany Free School."

—**Matt Hern, Ph.D.,** *editor of* Deschooling Our Lives

Making It Up as We Go Along

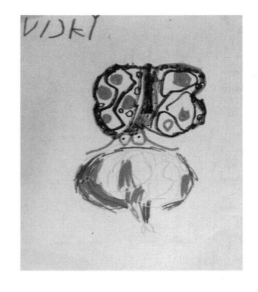

A student at the Free School draws from real life. At right, her rendition of the monarch butterfly that spent the afternoon posing on her shoulder.

Making It Up as We Go Along

The Story of the Albany Free School

Chris Mercogliano

Heinemann
Portsmouth, NH

Heinemann
A division of Reed Elsevier Inc.
361 Hanover Street
Portsmouth, NH 03801–3912

Offices and agents throughout the world

Library of Congress Cataloging-in-Publication Data
Mercogliano, Chris.
    Making it up as we go along : the story of the Albany Free School / by Chris Mercogliano.
        p. cm.
    ISBN 0-325-00043-3
    1. Free schools—New York (State)—Albany—History. 2. Free School (Albany, N.Y.)—History. I. Title.
LB1029.F7M47   1998
371.04'09747'43—dc21   97-51792
                                                                 CIP

Editor: Lois Bridges
Production: Abigail M. Heim
Cover design: Barbara Werden
Cover photograph: Connie Frisbee Houde
Manufacturing: Louise Richardson

Printed in the United States of America on acid-free paper

02   01   00   99   98   EB   1   2   3   4   5

To my mother, for teaching me about toughness and tenderness, and about truth in the face of dying. Walking with her to the gateway between heaven and earth helped me open the door to myself.

To Mary Leue, for her many years of mentorship, for her boldness of vision, which I hope is sufficiently described herein, and for her gentle nudging down the road toward my becoming a writer.

To all of the families who have made up the Free School and community over the years and to all of the teachers and students, past and present, for being my teachers and for generating the love, the compassion, the risk taking, the commitment, and the occasional outbreaks of zaniness thanks to which this story frequently told itself.

Last, but not at all least, to my beloved wife, Betsy, for all of her support, encouragement, and editorial help. And to our two beautiful daughters, Lily and Sarah, for putting up with me during these past two years of necessary preoccupation.

And finally, to the soaring spirit of children everywhere—may it live on in each and every one of us.

Contents

Foreword

This is one of the most unusual, extraordinary, and enlightening books I have had the privilege of reading, much less writing a foreword for. Mercogliano is a superb storyteller, and here he presents us with as profoundly important a view of education as is offered in our time. A certain sadness filled me, in fact, as I progressed into these chapters, for the message here is so essential to our children, selves, families, nation, and world. But what chance, I wondered, does this genuine pearl stand of being found in a landfill of trivia, bad ideas, and self-serving chicanery?

Not only does Mercogliano and his remarkable Albany Free School offer us a way out of the downhill spiral our schools are in, but, if we can hear him, he throws light on our personal dilemmas as well. His thesis runs seriously counter to our current chaos of conflicting ideas—ideas that push us like mad swine over a cliff. Yet I confess that some of his casual acceptances gave pause even to an anarchist and iconoclast like me. In every case, however, once I had considered his more revolutionary concepts, I saw how right, how dangerously right, he is.

Mercogliano and the Albany Free School teachers demonstrate a courage that is sobering. How many people truly put children's welfare ahead of self, reputation, public opinion, and pocketbook? How many of us stand outside our acquired prejudices and see children as they are, rather than as projections of our expectations? And how many of us are willing to look at our own dark side, which clouds our thinking about children? For, as

Carl Jung made quite clear, children live in our shadow side, our less-than-conscious fears and weaknesses that we hide from ourselves but can't conceal from them.

The teacher in the Free School is equally student, for leading children requires a fluid openness to the continually changing needs of the child, and a recognition of the great variation every child displays. This flexibility of approach is both demanding and risky. How safe, by contrast, are our educational systems, where the teacher's job is to demand compliance, judge the measure of such compliance, and, in effect, condemn if such demands are not met? Meanwhile, the Free School teacher must live into the moment with each child and respond according to that child's individual developmental needs.

As Mercogliano states and restates, "We spend much of our time attending to the emotional and interpersonal dimensions of everyday life in the school because we believe them to be the cornerstones of life and of all learning," a point current research heavily validates. And there we have the real issue. The Free School equips children for an actual life of interaction with others and one's own inner self; in the process, children learn—really learn—the same basics that most schools have such a fit over trying to teach.

As I look back on all the years of my life spent in a classroom, I can honestly say that—with the exception of learning to type in the ninth grade (the last actual grade I attended until college)—none of the nonsense I was commanded to learn—or else suffer lifelong consequences—had any meaning at all, then or since. None of it prepared me for anything actual, as assumed, nor in any sense did it equip me for life in the outside world.

What, I so often wonder, was that childhood thrown away for? My outrage, throughout those years, of the travesty inflicted on myself and children in general, has been confirmed continually ever since; I think that most children sense intuitively that the very fabric of their personhood is being violated by our current methods of child-care and schooling. I have no doubt that this is part of the reason for the undercurrent of rage in our land.

Getting a job fifteen years hence has nought to do with the seven-year-old building a structure of knowledge of the world and self, intent as he or she is on coming into dominion over that world as nature intended. Intriguingly, though, the subjects of the various chapters of this book do indeed suggest a kind of "curriculum" that is truly developmental. To my mind, Mercogliano covers the real and important matters of life, precisely those areas most of us were completely ignorant of when plunged into the marketplace as "educated" adults.

There are, after all, matters that *really* matter, such as interpersonal and intrapersonal relations; dealing with fear; concentration; the metaphors out of which we create our self-images and life stories; the issue of God, of which even young children are cognizant; race and class; sexuality; and that rarest of commodities, community. And how are such subjects taught? They are not and cannot be taught, only modeled and explored in the constant "chaos" of self-discovery around which childhood is based, and which is reflected, of necessity, in the Free School.

Which of us is willing to entertain the child's chaos so that the child can build his or her own unique structure of order, particularly through personal contact with us as subtle models? No, far easier to impose some abstract notion of preordained order on him or her, which we don't have to live up to but through which we can judge that child.

This book is a revelation, portraying the actual life of a child as I have seldom heard it expressed, and presenting a working format for leading children as they so desperately need to be led. Further, Mercogliano shows what can be done on a shoestring budget, literally a fraction of the amount being spent to no avail by public education. The Free School is truly a "therapeutic school" offering a model for our nation at large, were we courageous enough to accept the challenge.

I envy a first reading of this marvelously wise odyssey, and urge you not to dismiss what follows as unrealistic. We have no choice but to wake up and emulate the Free School's example, and discover, as with child development itself, the wonderful adventure of making it up as we go along.

—Joseph Chilton Pearce

Acknowledgments

I especially want to acknowledge the extended Free School community for their inspiration, suggestions, and encouragement, without which this first-time author never would have gotten out of the starting gate.

The many people who provided input and support along the way are too numerous to mention here, but I wish to thank all of you now. Special thanks go to Joseph Chilton Pearce, John Taylor Gatto, Ron Miller, Pat Farenga, John Lawry, and Jerry Mintz for convincing me I had a story worth telling.

I also want to thank my coeditors at *ΣKOΛE, the Journal of Alternative Education* and the *Journal of Family Life*—Mary Leue, Nancy Ost, Connie Frisbee Houde, Frank Houde, Ellen Becker, Larry Becker, Tom McPheeters, and Betsy Mercogliano—for helping me hone my writing skills and become a more effective communicator. Ditto to Heinemann readers Ralph Fletcher, Caren Black, Susan Harman, and Judith Larner.

For lending me the confidence to proceed when I didn't entirely yet possess it myself I am most grateful to Eve Ilsen, Paul Grondahl, Orm and Bunty Ketcham, Helene and Christy Chakos, Ram Dass, William Kennedy, Ivan Illich, Lee Hoinacki, and Matt Hern.

And very special thanks to my agent, Barbara Deal, and to my editor at Heinemann, Lois Bridges, for their unflagging faith in me and in this book.

Introduction

This is the story of a school. Actually, this is the story of certain children and adults who for nearly thirty years have been assembling under the guise of the artificial construct commonly known as "school." It is also the story of their interaction with the immense ground beyond school—with family, neighborhood, city, nation, race, class, and culture. For no school is an island, though many try hard to be.

A few years back, New York's statewide children's theater was in grave danger of losing its funding, all of which came from the state legislature. The Free School had been taking children to most of the group's productions ever since it had opened with *Peter Pan* ten years previously. A few of our students had even participated in its excellent program at one time or another. It was at the end of one of these plays that we were informed the theater would be shutting down when the season was over if its funds were not restored immediately. Upon our return, I overheard some of our older students (ages eight through twelve) discussing how upset they were about the loss of what they very much considered to be *their* theater.

I was equally upset, having witnessed year after year the incredibly positive impact that this kind of live theater has on children. I asked the students if there were anything they thought they might be able to do about the problem. Four students expressed a determination to at least try something, which led to a discussion of possible strategies. One suggested writing to the governor; another thought we should make signs and demonstrate in front of the state capitol; still another thought of contacting kids from other schools and asking them to write letters in support of the children's theater. All excellent ideas, but I explained to them that there was very little time and that it was actually the legislature that had the final say on the theater's funding—that the governor probably knew nothing about the issue—and since the current legislative session was nearly over, it was an excellent time to talk to individual legislators in person.

The students liked this idea, which was also a very practical one, since the legislative office building is only about ten blocks from our school. They asked me to be their appointment secretary. Before I made any calls, together we figured out which legislators to target. I then made one final suggestion: that the kids let the press know about their intentions, because a news story would surely bring further support for their cause. They liked this idea too, and asked me to serve as their press agent.

What followed were successful meetings with several influential legislators. I stopped attending after the first one, since the lawmaker seemed incapable of believing these kids had anything intelligent to say. Over and over he would address his remarks only to me. Not wanting to risk alienating him, we continued the meeting on his terms and then regrouped before the next appointment, which a local reporter was slated to cover.

The journalist was immediately impressed as he watched the students file into the legislator's office, leaving me behind in the waiting room. I detected a look of dismay on the elected official's face when I didn't get up and follow the kids in. As we had surmised, things went much better without me there. The reporter interviewed the four intrepid activists back at school; and lo and behold, the following Monday morning, every member of the New York State legislature arrived to find on their desks a copy of the *Albany Times Union* with the front-page headline: STUDENTS FIGHT TO SAVE NEW YORK STATE THEATER INSTITUTE.

Thanks to our efforts and to those of thousands of other concerned citizens across the state, enough of the theater group's funding was ultimately restored for it to keep its doors open. I could happily end the story here and leave you with the very accurate moral that kids can indeed make a difference even in today's complex world; but then you would be missing the real point. For that, the story needs two postscripts.

The aforementioned reporter's front-page story was brilliant, except for one not-so-small detail. I had brought a copy of the paper to school that morning and left it so the students could read about themselves while I went to make coffee. When I returned, three of them were elated; the fourth, Eliza, was totally bummed out—about what I could not imagine. When I asked her what was wrong, she showed me one of the story's opening paragraphs. The problem was all too obvious. Our reporter, trying to play the David and Goliath angle to the hilt, had set the scene by describing the four students sitting in the legislator's large leather chairs—especially noting how one girl's feet dangled short of the floor.

The operative word here was *short*, and this was where the article stopped as far as Eliza was concerned. The subject of physical size had become a sore one in this diminutive ten-year-old's life. I listened to her tell me about her hurt feelings, and then I asked her if it would help at all to share her reaction with the unknowing reporter. She thought about it a moment and said that it would, but then asked if I would tell him for her. I agreed and called him immediately.

Two days later, Eliza received a letter at school. It was from the reporter, who clearly had written it as soon as he had finished talking on the phone with me. He wrote that he felt especially bad about having focused on her small stature, because as a child he, too, had always felt embarrassed about being shorter than all the other kids. He also said that his reason for mentioning her size in the story was that he wanted people to be as blown away as he was by the hugeness of her actions. She was, he concluded, a giant in his eyes, and no doubt in the eyes of many of his readers.

After school, Eliza took the letter straight to her father's workshop, where he builds wooden boats, and together they made a beautiful frame for it. The letter now hangs proudly on a wall in Eliza's bedroom.

The second postscript unfolded a couple of days after the first. A *Times Union* columnist—the word *curmudgeon* must have been invented for this prickly old newsman—picked up on the story of the kids' lobbying efforts and attacked me and the school for "using the children as puppets" in what he saw as a blatantly adult political cause. Under the heading CRUSADERS EXPLOIT CHILDREN, he wrote that I, as their teacher, had no business manipulating them in order to pull on the heartstrings of the public and the powers that be. Children should be left alone to be children, he argued, for they would soon have plenty of time as adults to bear the world's burdens.

Needless to say, the students and I, along with the rest of the school, were outraged by the (also front-page) column, which happened to enjoy an enormous following. I volunteered to write a lengthy response, which the newspaper appropriately elected to print in its entirety in the Sunday edition op-ed page, adding to it the title WHEN CHILDREN AREN'T PAWNS. You get the idea.

This story ends about a week later with the receipt of a letter from the father of a student who had moved on from the school a number of years before. It read as follows:

Dear Chris,

I just read your article in the newspaper today discussing the issues Ralph Martin raised concerning the "use" of children in lobbying, protesting, etc. I would like you to know that I am in full agreement with your assertions and would like to thank you for your efforts.

Reading your thoughts in the paper brought me back to the days that my daughter Tiffany had the great fortune of attending the Free School. Your article is a reflection of the attention, commitment, and understanding that is so needed by the children of today's world.

Tiffany's transition to the public school system [it was this student's choice to switch to the school nearer to her small-town home] has been a great success. She has been maintaining superior grades every year. More importantly though, she has been self-motivated, secure, and working to her potential. Her teachers report that she is a wonderful student who participates positively in class.

There are times in everyone's life when perhaps we have doubts and insecurities as to what we are doing. Is it worth it? Am I doing it the right way? What does this mean in the end? I would like to take this opportunity to let the people at the Free School know that your work is invaluable, appreciated, and the effects generated by your endeavors are as a pebble cast into still water. The ripples go on in ways you will never know. Thank you so much and continue the great work.

Sincerely,

Laurence Thompson

THIS IS INTENDED to be a personal and intimate telling of the Free School's story, because it is a personal and intimate place. A similar consonance exists on another level: nowhere herein have I written up a soup-to-nuts description of the school's policies and philosophy, for that would be inconsistent with our underlying style, which tends to be too freewheeling and eclectic to fit into a conceptual nutshell. In other words, there is no pre-set methodology for me to describe because, day in and day out, we really do make it up as we go along.

For how can there exist a formula for this thing we so casually call "education" if one believes, as we do, that human lives are not externally programmed but are internally driven and directed? Call it fate, karma, the Holy Spirit, one's "higher power," inherited traits, the unconscious, or whatever you like—the force or forces that guide us from within are probably some unknowable mix of all of the above. But my goal in this undertaking will not be to try to unpack such an awesome mystery; rather it will be to render into words some of the possibilities that abound when forty-five or so children and eight or so adults choose to associate with one another under the same roof (or sky) in an atmosphere of freedom, personal responsibility, and mutual respect.

As you might imagine, a question frequently asked by baffled visitors is, "What is your school's structure?" I used to respond with long-winded, carefully crafted answers until it suddenly occurred to me one day that the "structure" of our little school in inner-city Albany, New York, is simply the ever changing host of people who make it up. No more, no less. It is the community of individuals—and here I mean *community* in the strictest sense of the word—who each day choose to participate in its unfolding. The school exists to be a medium for everyone's growth, the adults just as much as the younger people. In other words, the Free School is a living and dynamic context, not a static structure, technique, or philosophy.

But, some may wonder, how can kids learn to read and write and solve complex mental problems amid all of the messiness, noise, turmoil, and play? Do they achieve the same levels of competence as students in conventional schools? Absolutely. With one caveat: provided that the parents of children whose natural motivation has already been damaged by the antilearning tactics of conventional schooling or by too many antilife messages from the surrounding environment are willing to back off long enough for the necessary inner repair work to take place. Almost without exception, kids who have spent any significant length of time with us—with permission to learn according to their own rhythms—find themselves at least on a par with their peers if and when they enter a traditional classroom situation. Many, like Tiffany, whose father sent me the above letter, discover they are way ahead of the game. And all take with them a distinct advantage: while in the process of authoring their own experience at the Free School, they became competent, versatile, and independent learners.

Thirty years ago, the late George Dennison and his wife, Mabel, helped to start a short-lived school on New York City's Lower East Side called the First Street School. It was a radical experiment at the time because of the way it set out to practice real freedom and autonomy with ghetto children, many of whom were severely traumatized by the side effects of hard-core poverty. As George so compellingly described in his book, *Lives of Children,* their concept of school was not limited to being a place of instruction, but envisioned a comprehensively supportive environment geared to fostering growth in every human dimension. Above all else, they considered the field of relationships between the participants to be the locus of all real learning.

This meant that the First Street School was a passionate place, where the experience of love and deep caring—including conflict, anger, and even hatred—was considered primary. The Dennisons intuited then what is finally becoming accepted scientific truth now, namely that the heart is actually (and no longer only metaphorically) a central organ of intelligence, rivaling the brain in importance. When our founder, Mary Leue, started the Free School in 1969, the First Street School was one of her models; I think you will find as you read on that we, too, place the needs of the heart before all others.

One of our watchwords at the Free School, which hopefully will remain mine throughout, is Keep It Simple. Consider this paradox: The more data we gather about the human organism, the more we realize how extraordinarily complex it is, how greased the wheels are for growth and development, and how automatically growth and development will occur—unless someone, or some event, interrupts this natural process. And yet our systems of conventional schools, both public and private, grind on with their fear- and control-driven practices, refusing to take into account the fact that children, like all animal young, are inexorably programmed to learn.

Thus one of our primary missions at the Free School has been the debunking of the incredible mythology that has grown up around the basic functions of teaching and learning. The belief that education requires lots of money (the Free School's per-pupil expenditure is about one-fourth of the New York State average), sophisticated technology (we do very well with a few used microscopes and six hand-me-down personal computers), and extensive specialized training for teachers; and that learning to read and write, to become expressive and articulate, depends upon highly refined teaching and assessment methodologies—this is the stuff of a modern-day myth.

The nation's schools continue to serve as an easy target for our collective rage and discontent. In so doing, they absorb practically limitless quantities of dissent, thereby preventing us from seeing that the increasing dysfunctionality of our schools is merely one symptom of a much deeper disorder, one that Ivan Illich tried to put his finger on three decades ago in a series of radical critiques of American society.

The real culprit, according to Illich, is not the schools themselves; rather it is what he termed in *Deschooling Society* the "institutionalization of values." By this he meant an invisible process whereby our nonmaterial needs are transformed into demands for commodities. For example, health suddenly becomes dependent upon professional medical treatment, personal safety upon security systems and police protection, and education upon schools.

Here Illich warned that modern society has already successfully hatched a conspiracy to deny most young people open access to the secrets of the adult world, forcing them instead to run the maze of officially sanctioned licensing and training institutions if they are ever to realize their personal dreams.

Thus "education" becomes an insidious thing, another object to be consumed—something one must "get." I say insidious because most of us never even know what hit us—kind of like the lobster placed in a pot of cold water over a simmering heat. The chef doesn't need to cover the kettle, because the poor lobster never realizes it's being cooked. In other words, we two-leggeds are all conscripted into a massive schoolchildren's army long before we can veto such a move; and then as adults, the majority of us just as quietly and automatically hand the tradition on down to our children without ever questioning any of its basic assumptions.

The solution to this problem of abandoning our children to an institution that very often does not have their best interests at heart—by no means the fault of most teachers—is ultimately an internal one. Illich calls on us today to be constantly on guard against the myriad ways in which the culture tries to sell us the notion that we must "prepare our children for life" by seeing to it that their "educational needs" are "being met." Only in so doing will we ever stop mass-producing dependent people.

It is obviously going to take a concerted and conscious effort on all of our parts to turn the problem around. Fortunately, there is a measure of hope on the horizon, thanks in part to the recent resurgence of small, freedom-based schools like the Free School, and perhaps even more so to the homeschooling movement that is currently sweeping the nation. Now a million strong by some estimates, this largely leaderless phenomenon is busy demonstrating in very convincing fashion that learning doesn't require experts, that college entrance doesn't require prior formal schooling, and that successful and satisfying lives don't require college training.

I HAVE UNDERTAKEN this project with three broad goals in mind: to provide an in-depth history of the Free School, including a brief analysis of its place in the broader picture; to describe our school in a way that is meaningful both to those who have some point of reference to the various alternatives to conventional schooling and to those who do not; and finally, to address certain fundamental subjects like aggression, sexuality, race/class, and spirituality—four primary colors of human experience that are all too often relegated to the rusty side spurs of our national thinking about children.

You will find this book at times lighthearted and silly, because it deals with the lives of young children, who, thank God, prefer it that way. At other times, you will find it dead-serious and filled with fist-shaking outrage because it addresses certain issues that ultimately are life-and-death ones—the foremost being the fact that we have created a society that is carelessly throwing away so many young lives, sometimes with less than covert intent.

You will also find this book filled with my many personal biases. For instance, I am a rabid gardener, and a strictly organic one at that. And while I will do my best to resist the ever present temptation to turn life into a garden metaphor, you should know that my outlook is permanently infected by the organic gardener's creed: Always plant good seed and strong seedlings; maintain rich, healthy soil; make sure that everything gets enough air, water, and sunshine; talk or sing to your plants often; and otherwise relax, observe carefully, and intervene as little as possible, because the final outcome is beyond your personal control.

And then I am a Reichian, which means that I once immersed myself in the theories of the late Wilhelm Reich, a student of Sigmund Freud's, while at the same time I underwent several years of the kind of intensive body-oriented therapy that Reich developed over the course of his career. One of Reich's primary concerns was the prevention of excessive unhappiness (neurosis) by raising emotionally healthy children. He used the term *self-regulation* to underscore the importance of enabling children to recognize and meet their own needs and to set their own internal limits. Reich's concern with children led to a lifelong friendship and collaboration with the Englishman A. S. Neill, founder of Summerhill, which later became a model for a number of freedom-based schools around the world.

I have come to be influenced somewhat more recently by another of Freud's students, Carl Jung. From Jung I learned the value of examining life in terms of its archetypal and mythical dimensions. Jung's life and work stand as an indelible testament to the importance of considering the primary task of one's passage through this lifetime to be the creation of one's own personal myth.

I find myself, too, with a strong antiacademic bias. While hardly an anti-intellectual, having pursued a thorough post–high school education largely outside of any college classroom, I now have little regard for the academic world, filled as it is with symbiotic artificiality and self-serving trade lingo. Instead, my vision of education is grounded in living experience and is steeped in a personal faith that life inevitably creates its own lessons for us all.

I don't expect to have the last word on any of the issues I raise in the pages that follow. Instead, this book represents an attempt to provoke the questioning of certain entrenched perspectives as I weave together my personal outlook with some of the highlights of the Free School's continuing existence on one edge of the educational spectrum.

Again, it is my profound hope that it will be of value to parents or prospective parents of school-age children; to all who are engaged in the role of teaching or who are considering answering that calling; to individuals or groups who already have a school of their own or who are thinking about starting one; to those who are presently allowing their children's education to unfold at home or who are debating such a move in the future—to anyone concerned with the growth of healthy, whole children as we approach the twenty-first century at breakneck speed.

Making It Up as We Go Along

1

History

*T*he year the Free School started was the year of the Cambodia crisis, the student strikes, and the first Earth Day. Martin Luther King Jr. and Robert Kennedy had been assassinated the year before. These were indeed interesting times, when the birth of hope and the death of hope seemed on a collision course. And there we were, along with an uncounted number of other independent, experimental schools of all shapes, sizes, and micro-philosophies, determined to create genuine alternatives to the rigid, compulsion-based model of education that had been corralling the minds of American children for the past century.

As the Free School was taking shape in 1969, the diverse movement to bring about radical social change was more or less at its height. There was no unified agenda. Rather, the general order of the day was stopping the war in Vietnam, completing the work of the civil rights movement—especially eliminating the economic roots of racism—and breaking down the increasingly monolithic control of major social institutions such as the public school system.

This wouldn't be the first time in history (or the last) that among the activists attempting to bring about fundamental social change were those who believed that focusing on the prevention

1

of problems was equally, if not more, important than trying to solve them after the fact. Nor would this be the first time that the idealistic questions had been asked: What if we could raise a generation of children free of race and class prejudice, free of an overdependence on material things as the basis for the good life, and free of the belief in the necessity of war? And what if society were to begin embracing education as a process that encourages learning for learning's sake and enables children to develop fully and authentically?

Many, both in this country and abroad, have been addressing such fundamental questions for centuries. The family tree of the most recent attempts to radically alter the society's concept and practice of education, known first as the "free school movement" and later more euphemistically as the "alternative school movement," and now joined by the "homeschool movement," has many branches and deep roots. But anything more than the most cursory history of radical educational experimentation and change is beyond the scope of this book; thorough and excellent ones have already been written by Paul Avrich, Ron Miller, and others. My purpose here is to locate the Free School within the context of the larger movement from which it drew inspiration and to which it offers a certain measure of leadership, while at the same time viewing that movement in the larger historical context from whence it arose.

There were numerous common sources of inspiration. Certain schools, for example, chose to base themselves on the theories of nineteenth-century educational theorists like Maria Montessori and Rudolf Steiner, who believed human development to be guided by a spiritual force of some kind. Both believed, too, that all children have an innate desire to learn, and that it is therefore the task of education to nurture that desire through creative activity and direct experience. Finally, both considered the learning process to be far more than a series of abstract mental events, with Montessori tending more toward the sensory dimensions of intelligence, while Steiner, more esoteric in his thinking, homed in on the primacy of the imagination.

Ironically, while both dedicated their lives to the uncaging of the human spirit, both were responsible for the development of highly structured methodologies that sometimes leave little room for children's individual developmental needs. Meanwhile, the schools that their teachings have spawned—the majority of which have numerous points of agreement with mainstream middle-class cultural norms—continue to gain in popularity and numbers, in some instances even making inroads into the public system.

Other schools, far fewer in number, incorporated the ideas and ideals of either or both of the nineteenth-century countercultural paradigms, transcendentalism and anarchism. Two noted transcendalist philosopher-writers, Henry David Thoreau and Bronson Alcott, at one time founded schools of their own in which they set out to foster the spontaneous development of each child's natural gifts rather than the imposition of "knowledge" from the outside. Their ultimate goal was wholeness rather than merely mental or technical proficiency.

The radical political views of the anarchists led certain of their ranks to start their own schools as well, driven by the belief that the primary reason governments institutionalize education is in order to use it as a tool of social and ideological control. Furthermore, they believed that the surest route to a just society was to raise children according to just principles. Inspired by the writings of Kropotkin, Bakunin, and Tolstoy—who himself established a school for peasant children on his estate in his native Russia—the Spanish anarchist Francisco Ferrer started a short-lived school in Barcelona that ran from 1901 until 1906, when it was shut down by the state. It was named the Modern School, and its mission was to maintain an atmosphere of freedom in which children's inborn spontaneity would be protected and where children would learn to think for themselves. Ferrer made every effort to integrate middle- and working-class children, as well as girls and boys (coeducation was unheard of in Spain at that time). After his assassination by the government in 1909, the Modern School became the model for a number of schools in the United States.

Still other schools chose to imitate more contemporary radical school models such as A. S. Neill's Summerhill, founded in England in the 1920s. Though Neill steadfastly refused to sanction any followers, many nevertheless set out over the next half-century to adopt Summerhill's principles of freedom and democratic self-governance for students of all ages. The spread of "Summerhillian" schools continues today, and Summerhill itself is now run by Neill's daughter, Zoe.

Finally, in the 1980s, increasing numbers of families began withholding their children from the society's schools so that they could accomplish their learning at home, within the orbit of family and community and outside the hegemony of "government monopoly schooling," to quote John Taylor Gatto. They were guided by the writings of social thinkers like Ivan Illich and master teachers like John Holt—both of whom questioned the underlying idea of school in any of its forms. The homeschool movement, as it came to be known, is a truly grassroots phenomenon, essentially leaderless, and fiercely dedicated to the distinctions that Illich and Holt drew between "schooling," by which they meant a series of compulsory and artificial academic exercises, and real learning.

The typology for this broad new/old array of alternatives became as varied as the schools and households that chose to take up the experiment. "Humanistic," "free," "open," "new," "alternative," "holistic," "democratic," and "community" were some of the labels worn by the different types of schools. Some were more systematized than others; some tended to stress creativity and free expression while others concentrated on true democratic procedure; some were more academically oriented or carried a political agenda of one kind or another while others remained adamantly apolitical. "Homeschooling," "deschooling," and "unschooling" were some of the names given to home-based learning, with the latter two terms referring to a less formal method.

The stylistic differences between these various approaches to education were many; it was this very diversity that would become one of the unifying principles of the new freedom movement in American education. Spanning the broad spectrum of philosophies and ideologies was a single, underlying theme: there is no one right way to do it.

AMID THE UPHEAVAL and turbulence of the 1960s, the Free School was founded in 1969 by Mary Leue in the heart of New York's small, provincial state capital. For Mary this was an act of outright necessity. Recently returned from England with her husband and two of their five children, she watched her youngest son, Mark, becoming increasingly miserable in his fifth-grade class at one of Albany's better public schools. Mary made repeated attempts to address the problem with the teacher, the principal, and the school's PTA; all to no avail. Finally Mark refused to go at all; he asked his mother to teach him at home. Mary consented, and at that moment the Free School's basic operating strategy was born: Act first, get official approval later.

It wasn't long before Mary received a threatening call from Mark's principal, the school nurse having ascertained that Mark was no longer coming. This prompted Mary to attempt to establish the legality of teaching her son at home and led to the development of strategy number two: When you do seek out official approval, don't take no for an answer. Instead, keep cruising the bureaucracy until you locate that one "angel" who is willing to go to bat for your plan of action. Mary's persistence and determination paid off as she finally managed to find a man in the curriculum office of the State Education Department who assured her that she was well within her rights to educate her son at home. He offered to give her a copy of the "state guide-lines," which she could then present to any school official who might challenge her decision.

Sure enough, the local school district's truant officer called Mary the very next day and began issuing all sorts of final warnings. Mary calmly gave him the name of her newfound friend in State Education and not long after, the truant officer, who was actually the head of the district's Bureau of Attendance and Guidance, called back to apologize and to offer his assistance. Ironically, this man would later become the Free School's official liaison with the superintendent of schools, and a powerful ally. Thus, the first chapter of the Free School's story closed with Mark Leue becoming perhaps the first legal homeschooler in the modern history of New York State.

Two weeks later, Mary ran into a friend who had three children who were equally unhappy in school; she begged Mary to take them on. Not wanting Mark to be isolated with her at home, Mary agreed on the spot and at that moment, a school was born.

The rest of that initial year, to quote Mary, went swimmingly. As summer approached, Mary and her gang of four unanimously decided to continue the school for another year. They also agreed on a name for their new school, the same name it wears today. It was at that point that Mary began to step back and reflect on its future course. She visited other free schools, like Jonathan Kozol's Roxbury Community School in Cambridge, Massachusetts, and Orson Bean's Fifteenth Street School in New York City. She also read *Summerhill*, and struck up a correspondence with old Neill himself. At that time Mary was a member of a local group of civil rights activists who called themselves "the Brothers." She asked Neill what he thought of her idea of creating a school with Summerhill-style freedom for children of the inner-city poor. His inimitable response: "I would think myself daft to try."

Myriad influences from Mary's past also began to shape her vision for the new school. For instance, she had read the novels of Louisa May Alcott as a young girl and was fascinated by Alcott's descriptions of the school that her transcendentalist father, Bronson Alcott, had once operated. Also, Mary's grandmother had homeschooled Mary during what would have been her first-grade year. That early experience had reinforced in her Alcott's model of informal and self-directed learning, which incorporated large measures of free play and time spent immersed in nature. Mary's family, who lived near Concord, Massachusetts, even took swims in Walden Pond, made famous by the transcendentalist philosopher Thoreau.

Years later, while attending a Harvard University summer session, Mary was exposed to the ideas of nineteenth-century Russian anarchist Prince Kropotkin. Like many anarchists of his day, Kropotkin believed in allowing individual development to unfold naturally, and in freeing people from the straitjacket of a culturally conditioned point of view.

Finally, during her year in England, Mary had worked with David Boadella, a Reichian therapist who was the head of a small village elementary school at the time. In addition to her therapeutic work with Boadella, she studied Reich's voluminous writings and, like A. S. Neill, was particularly attracted to his theories concerning the healthy psychosocial development of children. All of these background influences would loom large as the Free School quickly took shape.

During that summer following the school's first year, Mary met with educational filmmaker Alan Leitman. He advised her to continue sifting through the realm of possibilities in order to find the approaches that would best suit her particular circumstances; and above all, to proceed slowly, making certain to complete one stage of growth before moving on to the next. Mary returned with three of Leitman's films about successful educational alternatives, which she then showed around the city to growing audiences. Suddenly, four students became seven, two teachers climbed aboard, and the need for a building was obvious.

A rapid and exhaustive search led to an inner-city black church in Albany's South End, which was moving to larger quarters across town. The minister agreed to rent the old building to the school for one hundred dollars a month. The deal accomplished two things: First, it gave the new school an affordable space. Second, the location ensured that the school would become well-integrated both in terms of race and social class. The rest of the summer was taken up with round-the-clock renovations and fund-raising. Come September, the Free School opened its doors for business.

What followed was a wild and tumultuous year. Parents battled over educational philosophy and practice, kids from opposite ends of the socioeconomic spectrum thrashed out their own issues, and several city departments (building, fire, and education) all vied to shut down this funky, radical, and penniless storefront institution. Once again, an ironic twist occurred within Albany's officialdom. As the bureaucratic noose tightened around the school's neck, and as the call to the city's mayor (who was nearing the end of his forty-two-year reign over a Democratic machine the power of which rivaled that of Chicago's infamous Mayor Daly) "to shut down that damned Free School once and for all" grew louder, it was Mayor Corning himself who came to the rescue, ordering his officials to work with Mary on whatever changes were called for. It wouldn't be the only time he would defend us, anarchists and hippies to the last.

Two important developments came out of that initial year of constant trial. First, teachers and parents hammered out, in a series of heated sessions, the policy that only those actually present in the building could determine the school's day-to-day operating policy. Others were welcome to attend meetings, and to advise and make suggestions, but that would be the extent of their power.

Next, in order to empower the kids to hold up their end of the bargain of "freedom not license," Neill's famous phrase from *Summerhill*, and also to give them a nonviolent way to work out their differences (which were many in that initial period), Mary and the others instituted a "council meeting" system. Accordingly, anyone who wanted to resolve a conflict or to change school policy could call a general meeting at any time. This enabled student and teacher alike to make new rules or change old ones, provided they could garner sufficient support for their position.

Council meetings proved to be an excellent forum for resolving conflicts between angry kids. And above all, they provided a solid sense of safety for all, acting as a kind of emergency brake whenever things got out of hand. When the focus was an interpersonal rift, meetings tended to take on a therapeutic rather than a governmental tone. They then became an empathetic space where emotions could flow freely and where the thread of the problem could be followed back to its source.

The council meeting system quickly became the heart and soul of the young school. It, more than anything else, would provide the wherewithal for the school to operate as a community in which everyone had an equal stake in the school and in which mutual responsibility and interdependence were daily realities. Also, students of all ages would grow adept at running the meetings in an orderly, coherent fashion, making council meetings an excellent form of leadership training.

The following year brought continued expansion and the need for a larger site. A new search turned up an old parochial school building situated in the old Italian section of the same South End neighborhood. At that time, the building was home to an Italian American war veterans group that had been the social center for a rapidly disintegrating immigrant community. Utilizing a small inheritance from her mother, Mary was able to buy it for practically a song from the veterans group, which was anxious to flee the influx of black and Hispanic newcomers.

The new building was perfect. Located in a row of solid four-story nineteenth-century brick row houses on a quiet side street, it had room to spare for the future growth that was soon to come. The first floor was already divided up into classrooms from the time that the building had served as a school. The largest of the rooms contained a new addition—a beautiful twenty-foot-long wooden bar, which would serve as a wonderful stage prop in many a drama during the early years. (The bar would later be sold to create more space and much needed cash.) The second floor consisted of a single open space, forty feet square, ideal for the kind of mixed-age preschool Mary had in mind. Already in steady use for more than a hundred years, the building was well worn and ready to accept the rough treatment it was about to get. Meanwhile, everything was in at least marginal working order so that no substantial additional funds were needed for renovations. To top it all off, the building came with a fully equipped commercial kitchen, enabling the school to participate in the federal free breakfast and lunch program and serve two good, hot meals a day.

With the addition of IRS tax-exempt status, the fledgling school began to take on a sense of permanence. Now it was time to tackle the two issues that would most profoundly determine its future—money and philosophy. Money wasn't an immediate problem, since the school's overhead was extremely low: Mary could manage on her husband's university professor's salary; the building was paid for; and the early teachers were able, at least initially, to work for little or nothing.

Nevertheless, the school was going to have to find a way to pay teachers a salary if it wanted to sustain itself in the long run. And the policy not to exclude any student for financial reasons—with tuition individually negotiated on a sliding scale based on income—certainly didn't help the situation. To make matters worse, Mary and the others were having no luck in getting grant money from private foundations.

Mary saw the failure to win grants as a mixed blessing of sorts. She knew that many of the new schools that went that route had folded up their tents as soon as their start-up grants ran out. Determined to set the school on solid financial ground, she decided to adopt Jonathan Kozol's suggestion that schools develop some sort of business scheme in order to avoid becoming tuition- or grant-dependent and therefore essentially restricted to white middle-class children.

The first two attempts at free enterprise—a college-textbook distributorship and a corner store—were both unprofitable. Then it occurred to Mary that a golden opportunity might be waiting literally right outside the school's front doors: with the neighborhood just about at its nadir, there were dozens of deteriorating buildings on the block for sale, cheap. Mary, using the remainder of her inheritance, bought a number of these sites for between $1,500 and $3,000 apiece. Altogether, the school has acquired ten properties. We gradually rehabilitated them ourselves, and now use them to house Free School teachers, families, and several adjunct enterprises. Much-needed financial donations are brought in, in return for the use of our properties.

Settling on the school's methodology proved to be an even more troublesome issue than money. Just like in the school's previous location, curious neighborhood children immediately began checking out our unorthodox operation—which had suddenly appeared to them out of nowhere and which bore little resemblance to school as they knew it. Since the only admissions requirements were parental consent and a good-faith effort to pay at least a little tuition, the student population of the school quickly reached a fairly even mix of middle-class and poor children. While this was wonderful in ideological terms, it presented the new school with a number of philo-

sophical conundrums, because as Mary and the other teachers soon discovered, the parents from the different socioeconomic groups tended to have
very different expectations regarding their children's schooling. Now it
would be necessary to learn perhaps the hardest operating principle of all:
You can't be all things to all people.

Mary and the other teachers, invoking the policy of absolute internal
autonomy, set out to cut a middle road through the forest of conflicting goals
and ideals. The working-class parents wanted the Free School to look and
function like the local public school, which virtually guaranteed their children
would remain trapped in the cycle of poverty. Their expectations were largely
governed by the values of a class system that had only betrayed them generation after generation, one based on upward mobility as a key measure of success. They wanted their kids to have desks, textbooks, mandatory classes,
competition, grades, and lots of homework. The absence of these trappings of
a "real" school became fertile ground for the fear that here their kids would
"fall behind," lose their competitive edge vis-à-vis the rest of society.

Mary, on the other hand, envisioned an egalitarian model in which kids
would be free of competition, compulsory learning, and social-class-based
status rewards. She thought that school should be a place where the students
could choose responsibly from open-ended sets of options, because only in
this way would they ever learn to chart their own life courses.

As one might imagine, getting this message across to a group of conservative lower-class white, black, and Hispanic parents was no easy task. Especially when the school's high-energy atmosphere, secondhand and thirdhand
furnishings, books and equipment, as well as the near invisibility of routine
all made it appear to them that we were not a school at all. It didn't help that
the word among kids on the street was that the Free School was a place where
kids could play all day, and also where they could curse!

To these doubtful parents, our school represented the fast track to failure and low status. Unable to cope with the uncertainty, sooner or later they
would end up putting their kids back in the public or parochial schools from
which they had come. In certain other cases, however, either the strength of
the personal relationship between these parents and the school, or of their
perception that at the Free School there existed a depth of human caring not
found in other schools, was enough for them to hang in with us long enough
to discover that their kids were growing in ways that would ultimately set
them free. Those who took that leap of faith quickly became heartened by
how totally their kids threw themselves into the daily life of the school. They
were equally impressed by the immediate improvement in their overall attitude toward learning and by their obvious jumps in maturity. A great many
of those early pioneering students still come back to visit today, and it is

wondrous to see how each has made his or her own unique way in the world. All are leading meaningful lives.

It was actually the upwardly mobile members of either social class who did most of the agitating for the school to be more formal than it had set out to be. They wanted proof that their kids were progressing in step with kids in the public schools. Parents for whom upward mobility was not a primary goal tended to be much more relaxed about the whole business. They were pleased by the behavioral and attitudinal changes they saw in their kids and were less concerned with homework, grades, and the like. For them, their children's happiness and sense of fulfillment here and now was more important than the promise of future rewards based on the society's predetermined scale of performance criteria.

"Discipline" was another area of potential polarization, and here the differences did tend to follow class lines. The middle-class parents generally wanted to see the school take a more laissez-faire approach, and when necessary, to set limits on children's behavior by reasoning with them or impelling them with adult-contrived incentives. The working-class parents, on the other hand, preferred strict enforcement of clearly defined rules of conduct, with punishment as the primary deterrent.

This same cultural dichotomy carried over to the controversial area of aggression, both its expression and its management. For many of the more liberal middle-class parents, aggression was practically a taboo, and they grew increasingly uncomfortable when they heard reports of fighting in the school. They liked the *idea* of sending their kids to a school with race and class diversity, but not the reality of exposing their kids to situations where occasional physical expressions of anger and sometimes rage were not ruled out.

In the end, it was decided that kids would be required to spend their mornings engaged in lessons and projects to improve their basic skills. Afternoons would be left open for kids to do more or less what they wanted—play indoors or out, paint, do ceramics, bang around in the woodshop, tend to the animals, visit parks and museums or any number of other interesting downtown locations. Boredom was seldom an issue. As the young school gradually gained confidence and experience, and as it established a certain respectability in the larger community, it would take a more and more relaxed approach to academic learning; but for the time being, the majority of the school's parents appeared to be satisfied with this initial compromise. It was then left to the teachers to contend with the sometimes mighty resistance of the kids who were already on the run from being compelled to learn to read, write, and figure in a school setting.

Mary was far less willing to compromise on the issue of aggression, and her Reichian influence was evident here. Reich's psychotherapeutic model had been based on the Freudian proposition that neurotic behavior and psychosomatic illness are in large part caused by the repression of certain urges, memories, and emotions. It was Reich who discovered that the energy of suppressed emotions is stored up in the body's muscle structures, which slowly rigidifies them and renders them less and less conducive to the flow of feelings, thus reinforcing the tendency to avoid emotional expression. The end result of this systematic blockage of energy, which Reich termed "armoring," was an inner sense of emptiness and isolation.

This, for Reich, was the taproot of the array of dysfunctional patterns that leads people to seek out the help of a therapist. In order to reverse the process, Reich added an active component to his form of therapy, something largely missing from the classical Freudian system. He got his clients up off of the couch to express, and if possible, to reenact, old, stuck emotions, believing that this was the fastest and most effective way to stimulate change.

Accordingly—and the fears of the middle-class parents notwithstanding—Mary was adamant that the Free School serve as a safe space where the expression of emotion would not only be permitted but would also, when appropriate, be encouraged. The school adopted a technique that enables kids to "rage it out." Here a willing and sympathetic adult holds a child who is ready to explode front-to-front on his or her lap and allows the child to safely struggle, kick, and scream until the energy of the rage is spent. Then can come forth the tears of pain and grief that are so often trapped beneath the anger. Many times over the years, I have seen children's armoring dissolve right in my lap after holding them in this way.

Also, it was decided not to outlaw physical fighting in the school. If two kids were determined to go at it in order to work out their differences—if the fight were fair and they weren't inflicting significant tissue damage on the other—then they were allowed to proceed, with an adult nearby to insure safety and if necessary, to help the combatants reach a mutual sense of completion and reconciliation.

Not surprisingly, given that the policy to permit fighting was such a radical one, it wasn't long before the school began to acquire a reputation in certain circles for "teaching fighting." The school's response to this spurious charge was to emphasize that there were numerous alternatives to fighting in place like the council meeting system, and that physical fighting was not all that common anyway. Furthermore, many mild-mannered children had sailed through the school without ever having had to lift a finger in defense of themselves. Mary talked about the importance of children coming to terms with what she called "the politics of experience," which the Free School, with its wildly heterogeneous mix of students, always seemed to offer in abundance. Thus the development of one's own personal style of self-assertion became an important learning task for everyone. On balance, the Free School quickly began to be noted for graduating children who displayed a self-confidence and a maturity beyond their years.

As it neared the end of its third year, the young school had managed to establish at least a bare-bones financial solvency and a mode of operation that seemed to have at least a chance of succeeding in the challenging mission that A. S. Neill would have thought himself daft to try. Growing pains remained intense. But the commitment to make it work shared by Mary, the other teachers, and core families was deep enough to keep everyone coming back.

As for Mark Leue, the reason it all began, he would move on through a progression of public and private schools until graduation from high school, try college for a semester and find it alien to his purposes, and then initiate his own training as a wood craftsman. Today he is one of the finest makers of stringed instruments in the state of Massachusetts.

MY WIFE-TO-BE, BETSY, and I arrived together in the late fall of 1973 to find a burgeoning school filled with adults and kids of all shapes, sizes, ages, and colors, about forty-five in all. Two naive and idealistic nineteen-year-olds, we had written to Mary the previous spring about the possibility of volunteering at the school, but wouldn't finally arrive until having spent the summer working to save money and then a few months gypsying around in an old Ford van.

At the time of the letter, I had been wrestling with the decision to withdraw from the southern university where I was a successful but frustrated liberal arts student. Two volunteer projects in which I was involved, one as a "big brother" to a ten-year-old black boy living in a dirt-floor shanty and the other as a tutor to a poor white boy of about the same age who was failing in school, had already begun to radicalize me in ways many of which I wasn't yet aware.

Soon I found myself independently reading books by John Dewey, Paul Goodman, A. S. Neill, Ivan Illich, Paulo Freire, John Holt, and finally Jonathan Kozol's *Free Schools*. It was Kozol's book that led us to Albany. He had included a listing of inner-city free schools, including Mary's, in the back of his book. When we wrote to each school on the list, every letter except one came back stamped "addressee unknown." That one was Mary's. Her response went something like, "You both sound neat. Why don't you come and visit. We don't have any money, but maybe we can give you a place to stay."

The Free School turned out to be exactly what we were looking for. The year before I had filed as a conscientious objector with the draft board (although the Nixonian draft lottery would ultimately exempt me anyway), and so volunteering at the school became for me a sort of unofficial alternative service. Betsy, who had worked with kids in various capacities while she was in high school, quickly discovered that she was a natural teacher. Later, after completing nursing training at a local college, she would become the school nurse as well.

I was excited to find the school located in a rough-and-ready, racially and ethnically mixed ghetto neighborhood, where it was as involved in dealing with the reality of inner-city poverty as any government-sponsored Vista project. And better still, unlike Vista, the Free School wasn't doing anything *for* anyone, but rather *alongside* them. After an exploratory visit, Betsy and I returned right after the Thanksgiving holiday and moved into a minicommune for teachers, interns, and volunteers housed in one of the school's newly acquired four-story flats.

All of the initial teachers had arrived in more or less similar fashion. Bruce had been the first to join Mary. Having just quit his public school teaching job in protest over the firing of a colleague for the high crime of growing a beard, he heard about the Free School from Mary's eldest son. Tall, easygoing, and mustached, Bruce plunged headlong into developing the new school, working evenings and weekends as a church sexton in order to keep the wolves from his and his wife's door.

Next to arrive was Barbara, with her two young children in tow. An Albany native, Barbara had no formal teaching experience, but was an excellent mother, and, like Mary, a formidable presence. Having already completed her hippy pilgrimage to Berkeley, California, she had recently returned to put down roots of her own in her hometown. Together, Bruce and Barbara would tackle the job of establishing a preschool program in the building's upper story, which grew rapidly due to the acute need in the neighborhood for affordable child-care.

Then came Lou, and then Rosalie. Both were Italian American and both were in retreat, to one extent or another, from their Roman Catholic upbringings. Like Barbara, Lou was a native of Albany and had actually grown up in the same neighborhood as the school. One of the first things Lou did was to move in the antique pump organ that had belonged to his grandfather. This added a particularly karmic touch to the building, which for its first forty years had been a Lutheran church built by German immigrants. No doubt there were ghosts smiling in the rafters as they listened to Lou's early-morning preludes.

Rosalie had just spent a year teaching children on an Indian reservation in North Dakota, and before that, two years at a parochial school in her native Bronx. She would later parlay her experience at the Free School into a master's thesis on the relationship between the ideas of John Dewey and Jean Piaget and their practice in an inner-city free school environment. Rosalie had no plans for children of her own and the kids soaked up her gentle, doting style like dry sponges in warm water. Perhaps not so ironically, the school proved to be a magnet for renegade Catholics, myself included.

Such was the central group of full-time teachers who greeted Betsy and me when we showed up. Numerous others—volunteer parents, college interns, itinerant young people, neighborhood characters, foreign visitors—had come and gone, and would continue to come and go, each contributing in his or her own way to the school's constantly changing flavor.

MEANWHILE, THE SCHOOL was growing more intense than ever. Many of the students and their families were in crisis much of the time, and all of us who were working in the school full-time found ourselves living on the edge. Salaries, when we got paid at all, were minuscule, and survival became one of the overriding reasons for a number of us to continue living together communally in school-owned housing—a dimension that added greatly to the school's interpersonal froth.

Working closely with the kids inevitably brought teachers face-to-face with their own unresolved childhood issues. Many of us had grown up in dysfunctional families ourselves, and several had suffered various degrees and forms of abandonment or abuse. All of us felt extremely challenged by the intimate depth and the emotional content of the relationships in the school—children with children, children with adults, adults with adults.

It gradually became apparent that some sort of supportive forum was needed in which the adults could resolve conflicts and deepen their understanding of themselves and of each other. Mary suggested that we start a weekly personal-growth group where we could both clear up unfinished *inter*personal issues and safely delve into areas of *intra*personal growth.

Our four-hour Wednesday-evening group has now been meeting continuously since 1974. Its inception marked the first in a series of organic steps toward the birth of a permanent community surrounding the school. Part therapy and support group, part conflict-resolution setting, part community meeting, "group," as we call it, remains an absolute cornerstone of both school and community, and unquestionably is the key to the longevity of both. It is here that we continue to sharpen our "humanity skills" by attempting to practice emotional honesty through compassionate confrontation both with the truth and with each other.

Over the next few years, we all threw ourselves with abandon into improving the school, the buildings that it had been steadily acquiring on the block, and ourselves as well. Thanks to our remaining Italian neighbors, and to many other longtime working-class black and white residents, the neighborhood in which the school now found itself had a villagelike quality. It was to this well-established base that we began to add our own countercultural accent.

We would soon discover one of the real blessings of this Old World type of neighborhood: Though not without its prejudices, it will quite readily accept personal differences as long as they are presented without pretense. This would be proven out in the warm months, when the real business of our neighborhood is carried out on the "stoops," or high front steps of each building. In order to establish good neighborhood relations, we made a point of spending ample time visiting with neighbors on their stoops. Today, we are well-accepted members of the larger community, having at times been strong advocates for issues such as home ownership for poor people during the period of rampant gentrification that took place in the mid-1980s.

The teachers who stayed on at the school began settling into more permanent relationships and also began spreading out into the various Free School buildings. Because the buildings were on two parallel streets, they often had adjoining backyards. With the buildings more or less in order, we started improving the yards, creating cooperative gardens and outdoor gathering places. More and more, we found ourselves eating together, celebrating birthdays and holidays, and even twice mourning together, after the stillborn deaths of Betsy's and my first two baby girls. Though no one quite realized it at the time, this closely shared living and working represented another seed of community, one that was already sprouting.

Teachers began having their own children (Betsy subsequently gave birth to two wonderfully alive daughters), and with them came the urge to put down still more permanent roots. Following the school's earlier example, we began buying our own abandoned houses on the block. Betsy and I purchased one for five hundred dollars, though at the time it wasn't much more than a leaking roof over a hole in the ground. Equipped with the necessary skills and tools, but still with no money to speak of, we devised a cooperative system for helping each other with our houses, often by means of weekend-long "work parties," as we called them. For example, once, on two successive weekends, we had an Amish-style barn raising in our backyard and completed a two-story barn and hayloft over the course of those four days. The barn now houses three Alpine dairy goats, which students learn to milk, and two dozen or so laying hens, to whom we feed the leftovers from the school's free breakfast and lunch program. This sharing of skills and labor contributed dramatically to the sense of community that was now becoming quite perceptible.

It was also during this period that Mary, with assistance from Betsy (who dreamed of becoming a midwife and is a fine one today), started the Family Life Center. The new spinoff was a response, in part, to the Free School's own "baby boom." Its purpose: to offer counseling and prenatal care to pregnant women, to provide parenting support, and to teach medical self-care to young families.

The Family Life Center provided the opportunity for the first of many synergistic exchanges between the school and its offshoots. In addition to creating an internal source of support, the center immediately began attracting new families to the school and to the budding community. Soon, two "center families" got wind of what we were up to and bought houses on the block.

These center families would go on to send their kids to us at age two or three, and the school would thereby reap a further benefit from the births that Betsy and Mary were facilitating. We could see immediately that center children seemed to be in generally better shape than the children who were products of standard, mechanized hospital birth procedures. Current research in neonatal development is now confirming our earlier observations. Numerous studies show that newborns who are allowed to bond fully with both mother and father immediately following birth demonstrate much higher developmental curves than those who are not.

Now the influence of Kropotkin-style anarchism on Mary's thinking very much entered the foreground. Born just after World War I into a New England Yankee tradition of staunch self-reliance, Mary was appalled at the current generation's increasing dependency on experts. Like Kropotkin, she saw the need for people to return to living in small, sustainable communities where they could learn to work together to develop their own localized support systems tailored toward specific needs. It was Mary who first suggested that we organize ourselves into an intentional community.

Along with home ownership and growing families came the need to stretch what little money each of us had, as well as to be able to borrow it at affordable rates. Here Mary had the idea of pooling as much capital as each of us could individually afford, so that we could invest it jointly in order to earn higher rates of interest on savings and simultaneously create a capital fund that could be loaned out. The interest payments would then get reinvested, thereby "keeping the money in the family." Mary named this joint venture "Money Game." Today, its assets are not insubstantial.

Also during this period, we launched two additional spinoffs, one primarily for internal support, the other external. Mary and Nancy, a teacher who arrived not too long after Betsy and me and who was the first to give birth in the Family Life Center, had both started natural food stores in the past; together they decided to collaborate on a small co-op in the basement of the school's Family Life Center building. Mary soon added a bookstore to the operation; a few years later, Connie, a costume designer and longtime community member, opened an adjoining community crafts cooperative and storefront.

In order to help low-income Free School families take the same low-cost, "sweat equity" route to home ownership that many of the teachers had followed, we established a revolving housing-loan fund and rehabilitation-assistance group. We were able to bring together enough private investors to enable us to issue mortgages at low interest rates. Drawing on our accumulated skills and experience, we then taught families inexpensive ways to rehab their homes, doing as much of the work themselves as possible.

Our growing alliance gradually gained more definition as we moved together through the decade of the 1980s, when we began to refer to ourselves simply as the "Free School community." With the school buildings and our homes more or less completed, and with all of the various community projects up and running, next we turned toward spiritual matters. Having come from a wide variety of religious backgrounds—primarily Jewish, Roman Catholic, Protestant, and Buddhist—we found ourselves sharing with each other the prayers, practices, and holy days we had carried forward into adulthood. We also began borrowing from other systems, particularly various Native American and ancient matriarchal rituals. And while we maintained our own spiritual identities, we each were nourished by this evolving shared tradition.

This added spiritual dimension contributed heavily to the permanence and vitality of the community of the now dozen or so families that had gradually rooted themselves in varying proximities to the school. At the same time that there was an ongoing exchange between the two, the Free School community began to establish a life of its own independent of the school proper.

BOTH SCHOOL AND community continued to evolve as people came and went, and as we added new dimensions. Certainly the most significant of these changes occurred in 1985, when Mary retired from daily teaching in order to establish a quarterly journal that would help to spread the ideas and accomplishments of the educational freedom movement she was devoting the last half of her life to. Borrowing the classical Greek word for *school*, she named it *ΣΚΟΛΕ* [pronounced sko-lay, the ancient Greek word for school], *the Journal of Alternative Education*. Over the years *ΣΚΟΛΕ* has developed a strong international following of readers and contributors and its influence continues to expand.

Not long afterward, Mary decided it was time to pass on the director-ship of the school. First the torch was passed to Barbara, then to Betsy and me as codirectors, and when Betsy left to become a full-time midwife, to Nancy and me. The transition was not without its difficulties. However, thanks in part to the support and commitment of the surrounding commu-nity, effective new leadership is in place, with Mary continuing to play a valu-able role as a mentor and advisor.

The success of *ΣΚΟΛΕ* led Mary to envision a second quarterly maga-zine that would address the broader needs of families, incorporating the Free School's wide range of experience with issues beyond the ordinary confines of education. Today, the *Journal of Family Life,* as well as *ΣΚΟΛΕ,* are pro-ductions of the Free School community as a whole.

Realizing that all work and no play makes dull boys and girls, we decided we needed a place where we could get away from the city occasion-ally. Larry, a community member with a knack for finding bargains, man-aged to find a camp for sale on a small lake about twenty-five miles east of Albany, in the foothills of the Berkshire Mountains. (In upstate New York, *camp* refers to a vacation cottage or home in a wooded or waterfront area.) With two forty-foot living rooms, six bedrooms, and two kitchens, and an owner willing to sell for a low price because the building was in need of sub-stantial repairs, it was exactly what we were looking for. We practically bought it on the spot!

Today Rainbow Camp, as we christened it, is a multipurpose facility, used by the community for retreats and vacations, by the school for daylong and weeklong trips with the kids, and by Rainbow Camp Association (com-posed of members of the Free School community) for its weekend workshop program. The workshops cover a wide range of topics in the general area of personal and spiritual growth, and workshop themes and leaders are usually chosen with the needs of our souls and psyches in mind. Any profits from the workshops go toward paying for camp improvements and taxes.

The purchase of Rainbow Camp led to a friendship with Hank Hazleton, a retiree living on 250 acres just over the hill from the camp. Hank was busy devoting the remainder of his life to defending the rights of Native Americans when he suffered a series of crippling strokes. He had yet to realize his dream of turning his land into a wilderness education center and a forever-wild sanc-tuary. To the Free School's great good fortune, before he died Hank willed his land to us so that we could assume its stewardship and carry out his vision. Currently, we are finishing a twenty-four-foot-diameter octagonal "teaching lodge" in a small clearing in the forest, and with the help of the Audubon Soci-ety of New York State we are in the process of establishing a wildlife sanctuary. A ropes course with both low and high elements is also in the works. Eventually we hope to convert Hank's house and barn into a small quasiresidential adjunct for Free School students.

As this unusual school urges itself forward, its future course is still largely uncharted. At every turn along the way, the development of the Free School and community has been essentially organic in nature. At no point has there been a master plan or a single guiding philosophy or model; rather, at every step, function and necessity—with occasional outside inspiration— have dictated form and process. With money in short supply, we've had to become our own experts, hashing out our own solutions, learning from our many mistakes. As both school and community grow and evolve to meet changing times and circumstances, the challenge remains for us to live out, on a daily basis, the basic principles of love, emotional honesty, peer-level leadership, and cooperation, which are the heart of the Free School's concept of education.

2

Mumasatou

Mumasatou! Mumasatou!
Mohammed's child queen,
Jewel-eyed princess,
Africa Dream maiden.
Rageful, willful,
Full of fire;
Three-year-old skin
Stretched taut over terror.
You cut dream monsters
Into tiny pieces,
So those scissored demons
Will haunt you no more.
You are alive!
Total!
Your chariot races the dawn
Across Sahara sands.

Jolofe warrior's child;
L'enfant sauvage
Born in a Brooklyn jungle.
You learned to say,
"Shut the fuck up,
Bitch!
Hell No,"
When you mean,
"SEE ME!

HEAR ME!
STOP ME!
Be for me; be for real."
Always probing for the center . . .
"ATTENTION EVERYONE!
I AM MUMASATOU!
Ignore me at your peril!!"

*S*he arrived at our door unannounced, three years' worth of rompin', stompin' hell's-on-fire. Since the Free School is an energetic place to begin with ("How do you people stand the noise?"), and since Mumasatou was obviously a tightly strung, high-energy kid, we knew from the outset we were about to have our mettle thoroughly tested.

As soon as the dust began to settle, two questions emerged: What did this unusual child need and what had she come to teach us?

Immediately, our lightning-fast, captivating little girl showed us that she needed limits and protection—plenty of both. Virtually uninterested in the other children, she possessed a seemingly inexhaustible repertoire of tricks for winning the attention of every adult in the Big Room, as we call the large open space that houses the preschool. Her favorite: dashing over to any nearby table with stuff on it—preferably breakable—and with one sweeping motion of her arm, seeing how far she could launch the whole mess, smiling at you all the while.

Kids raised in an interpersonal economy of scarcity will always choose negative attention over no attention at all; unfortunately, negative attention can become quite addictive. Mumasatou was the ninth of ten children (now eleven, with the addition of an older sister's baby), with a father who travels from Africa to visit them briefly once or twice a year. Her mother is an intelligent and competent woman who is doing the best she can, but who readily agrees that "The Old Woman and the Shoe" could have been written about her family. It's not hard to see how Mumasatou has been forced to scratch, scrape, and connive for the love she needs to develop fully.

Better disguised is the silent deprivation growing to perhaps epidemic proportions in the millions of "average families of four" across late-twentieth-century America, leaving our schools with an almost hopeless caretaking task as they are increasingly flooded with "damaged goods," as Joseph Chilton Pearce so bluntly puts it.

It wasn't long before we had run through all of our tried-and-true methods for socializing such radical free spirits as Mumasatou, and realized that it was time to punt. This little she-tiger was not about to roll over and adapt to our enlightened program. The strategy we fell back to was a simple one: Nancy, a twenty-year veteran of the school who had four kids of her own, began to hold and rock and carry her around for much of the school day. A very physical child, hungry for affection, Mumasatou immediately began lapping up the one-on-one contact like a kitten with a saucer of milk.

Along with the consistent limits that would help her learn ways to get positive attention, Mumasatou required protection. She was initially so prone to sudden rage, and such a fearless fighter—all teeth and claws—that she needed us to keep her, and the other kids, safe from her out-of-control impulses.

Children who are frequent biters contain a lot of fear, and Mumasatou's own rage and fear terrified her at times. She had lived the first two years of her young life in a public housing project in the war-torn Fort Green section of Brooklyn, where shootings were a daily occurrence. Whenever Mumasatou bumped her head, she would immediately grab it with both hands and shriek inconsolably, "I'M BLEEDING!! I'M BLEEDING!!" I never quite figured that one out, though it is finally being recognized that certain ghetto children are actually suffering from Post-Traumatic Stress Disorder—the name given to the set of potentially disabling psychiatric symptoms found in returning war veterans. I am certain that this was true of our little *enfant sauvage*, the title Francois Truffaut used for his classic film about a boy who was raised by wolves.

Being with Mumasatou early on could be exhausting, both physically and emotionally. Nancy, who is as stalwart as they come, eventually reached the point where she just couldn't give her anything more; I volunteered to take the next turn.

I quickly learned several things. First of all, Mumasatou had extremely thin boundaries between herself and her environment, much like a newborn infant. She was ever so sensitive to the moods and feelings of those around her, to whatever was "in the air" at a given moment. Also, I found that changes—even subtle ones—and transitions of any kind, especially beginnings and endings, were very difficult for her.

When I began to put Mumasatou down on the floor and encourage her to play and explore, it was obvious that I was going to have to monitor her moods and excitement level. She was utterly incapable, at first, of regulating them herself. At this point Mumasatou's only way of modulating her energy was to work herself up into a tantrum, again much like a newborn infant. My goal became to gather her back in before this would happen, and to slowly help her build up a repertoire of less dramatic alternatives that would enable her to wind down gradually and, if possible, independently from me.

Toward this end, Mary loaned us her irresistibly huggable, oversize teddy bear, which we kept on hand at all times. Mumasatou learned she could calm herself by sitting and rocking with Dr. Bear (he wears a physician's shirt) whenever she started to lose control. It is very important for young children to develop the ability to quiet their inner fears on their own, and so we almost always encourage the establishment of relationships between them and their "loveys," as Harvard pediatric expert T. Berry Brazleton calls the stuffed creatures that kids sleep with, take places, and so on.

Thanks to Nancy's steadfast presence early on, before long I was able to start weaning Mumasatou from my constant attention. Looking back, I am convinced it was the initial total-body contact, with both a woman and a man, that was the key that unlocked the inner room in which Mumasatou had felt so trapped. We were thrilled to watch her begin to speed through some of the early developmental stages she had skipped for one reason or another.

Mumasatou began taking little steps out of her private world, with plenty of medium-range supervision from me. She even began, very tentatively at first, engaging in play with some of the other three-year-olds. Fortunately, we had a couple of little girls that year who were live wires themselves. They were undaunted by Mumasatou's frequent attempts to dominate and a healthy respect grew up between them. I tried to stay out of this process as much as possible, sometimes having to bite my lip when the fur began to fly. Thankfully, by this time Mumasatou's propensity to search and destroy had mellowed into a more sociable kind of aggression that the other children could generally handle by themselves. When they couldn't, I would intervene, like a lifeguard swimming them out of the deep water of their more violent urges to where they could stand again, and then talk, or yell, or scream things out.

As the end of the school year approached, Mumasatou was able to spend longer and longer periods on her own. This meant—much to my relief—that I could turn her over to the other preschool teachers and take care of some of the school business I had been neglecting.

BESIDES BEING A beguiling, demanding child, Mumasatou became for me a kind of living metaphor—hence the inspiration for the poem that begins this chapter. I am more convinced every day that we all have a willful, wild child inside of us, an opportunistic kid who can't wait to dart out and steal the show when no one's watching. A wily rascal like this sees itself as all powerful and as the absolute center of the universe. I know I have one inside of me.

Some of us, I think, have more luck reckoning with this urgent inner force than others; most, I have noticed, tend to swing wide in one direction or the other: either we end up trying to squash the little bugger flat—and then take life altogether too seriously—or we let it run wild—and then spend a great deal of time and energy extricating ourselves from one kind of trouble or another.

Isn't struggling with such conundrums the stuff of which life is made? Every major spiritual or psychotherapeutic system, Eastern or Western, attempts to address this powerful and generally antisocial part of us that just wants what it wants when it wants it—to hell with anyone else—and each varies in its prescription for dealing with it. Many refer to it as "the ego"; some capitalize the *e* and some don't.

For the time being, I'll call this inner construct the "Mumasatou principle." On the one hand, it is a plentiful source of human vitality and creativity; on the other, it is practically begging to know that there exists some force greater than itself. In other words, it simply needs to know that it can be stopped when necessary. Few things are more frightening to young children than perceiving that they have too much power.

One of the Achilles' heels of my generation has been our opposite-extreme reaction against the often rigid and authoritarian child-rearing practices of our parents' generation. The Free School is about as racially and ethnically mixed as a small school can be, and I have seen this trend extend across the lines of race and social class. It is my observation that there are a lot of kids running around today who are being fed a diet too rich in power, and this problem gets further complicated by the fact that many of my peers would just as soon dismiss or avoid issues of either personal or political institutional power. I certainly have had to learn a number of hard lessons here while raising my own two children.

I knew a woman in her early fifties who had to be removed from her home against her will because it was determined that she had become "a danger to herself or others." This painful turn of events occurred at the end of a very long, very hard winter during which she had been heroically providing twenty-four-hour care for Hank, the now bedridden old man who had titled over his land to the Free School when he fell terminally ill.

I had known Hank's nurse for several years and, alarmed by her increasingly bizarre behavior and by Hank's rapidly deteriorating condition, had been encouraging her to seek outside help, which unfortunately she was convinced she didn't need. Finally, when she persisted with a series of violent rages and outbursts at would-be supporters and visitors, a local judge ordered her to undergo a seventy-two-hour psychiatric evaluation—which she was also convinced she didn't need.

My reason for telling this story has to do with what I observed as two state troopers and later the local rescue squad attempted to get the nurse to come to the hospital with them. She was certain that those seven men and women, who remained impressively calm and patient for as long as was humanly possible, lacked the wherewithal to get her out of that house. At several points she even verbalized her conviction that she was more powerful than the lot of them combined, and I stood by in awe as she ran through an amazingly artful assortment of maneuvers to delay the inevitable. Ultimately, the authorities were forced to capture her physically and carry her, strapped to a stretcher, out to an ambulance.

I include this story as a defining example of what I mean by the "Mumasatou principle," in this case in an adult well into the second half of her life. Not surprisingly, as a young child Hank's nurse—like three-year-old Mumasatou—had not received adequate nurturing from her mother. Being stopped in that way, as awful as it was, turned out to be just what she needed in order to return to herself. She was released immediately following the seventy-two-hour period, having received no treatment or medication whatsoever, and was able to resume her much needed caretaking role.

MUMASATOU RETURNED TO us the following September as full of it as ever. Thankfully, so did her two equally strong-willed cohorts, Ashley and Tiara. The three would become thick as thieves this year, and it was fascinating to watch Mumasatou struggle with the everyday give-and-take of friendship. It didn't come easily. Her ever present desire to get her own way—hardly atypical at this age—would continue to be the biggest stumbling block to any real intimacy with her peers.

I gradually came to realize that a great deal of Mumasatou's antisocial behavior was habitual, stemming from the combination of her inborn demanding temperament and the effects of living in a crowded family, in a crowded apartment, in a crowded inner-city neighborhood, always with another new baby around to monopolize most, if not all, of her mother's attention. The effects of growing up on one of the bottom rungs of a tall ladder full of siblings constantly telling her what to do and when to do it (NOW!) were readily apparent.

Unfortunately for the teachers and the rest of the kids, aggressing against others remained Mumasatou's preferred way of releasing pent-up anxiety and frustration. Here there was little for us to do but sit back and let the chips fall where they may. Friendship cannot be taught, only prevented—by keeping kids too busy to interact with each other naturally; by setting them one against another with grades, tests, and special privileges; and by perhaps the simplest of all means, age segregation.

Children in our preschool, and the older kids for that matter, often spend a good part of each day engaged in self-structured play. They also paint and dance and sing along to tunes Lori joyfully beats out on the school's sturdy old upright. They read and are read to, and they learn their letters and numbers and how to write their names. They bake cookies and bread and make butter from fresh cream. These kinds of activities, of course, are structured by the teachers. Kids partake when they so choose.

Mostly they play in a world of their own creation, and the teachers move about the periphery, where the kids can seek us out as needed. We do it this way for many reasons. The first is that children are constantly learning on a myriad of levels while they play—about time and space and proportion, about the power of language, about themselves and each other. But perhaps the most important reason is that even three- and four-year-olds will frequently form very tight bonds with each other if given the chance to associate freely and to discover their own ways of working out their differences. The same is true of two-year-olds, and also of infants. Add the notion of "parallel play" to my personal list of modern-day myths. It is simply another end product of the ethos of scientific child-management upon which conventional schooling so self-assuredly rests.

On her good days Mumasatou was a social butterfly. She would merrily play house with Ashley and Tiara for hours on end. Together they dressed up in elegant gowns and bedecked themselves with jewels and crowns of all kinds. They joyously paraded around in their huge, high-heeled pumps, until the constant clicking became unbearable (for the teachers). They groomed baby dolls ad infinitum, prepared them imaginary meals made out of clay, and rocked and read them stories. In this way, Mumasatou gradually grew more tolerant of the needs and demands of others.

Mumasatou would be the first to wrap her skinny brown arms around a new visitor. She was the best ambassador we'd had in years, quickly making guests feel at home with her engaging smile and a string of who, what, where, and why questions. Soon she became quite attached to Richard, a carpenter in the community who did a lot of the ongoing renovation work on the school's buildings. Most days they could be found sitting together at one of the lunch tables, engaged in animated conversations, her squarely in his lap.

On her bad days she would arrive at 8:15 with a dark, defiant look on her face, which only meant trouble. All I could figure was that her entire household must have gotten up on the wrong side of the bed on mornings like this. Or she would come in with stories (always true) about someone breaking into their apartment and throwing a knife at her older sister, or about the cops dragging away her brother for selling drugs.

Mumasatou tended to revert to her violent ways on these days. While we were having some luck getting her to verbalize her volcanic emotions rather than lash out at others, there were still times when the only thing to do was wrap her up so that she could safely rage and cry it out.

By now we had learned that when Mumasatou was this far out of sorts she was much more at ease playing outdoors or in the quiet of one of our homes, or alone painting or working with Play-Doh or clay. Sylvia Ashton-Warner once made the same discovery during her first year as the only teacher in a village school for children of the Maori, the indigenous people of New Zealand. The Maori were at that time a warrior tribe, and hence their children were volatile and hot-blooded, much like our Mumasatou. Ashton-Warner wrote a masterpiece about her extraordinary experience entitled *Teacher*. Here she coined the terms "creative vent" and "destructive vent" to explain the dramatic transformation that took place in her little one-room school, once she stopped adhering to the rigid British-style curriculum she was told to teach and instead provided the kids with the means to draw and paint and build and create books of their own, using *their* images and *their* words.

Ashton-Warner's insight needs little explanation. As long as she insisted on trying to control the natural passion of her students with external discipline and endless routine and busywork, their abundant energy inevitably found its expression in one destructive act or another. When the kids weren't fighting, they were busy tearing apart the classroom she had worked so hard to create. But when she opened up the creative vents of art, music, poetry, and dance, the violent behavior virtually disappeared.

And so it was with Mumasatou. The more we helped her find creative outlets, the less we had to restrain and control her. And always it was crucial that we recognize her positive attributes. Just like the Maori children, her natural aggressiveness was a double-edged sword. Here's a prime example: One day I took Mumasatou and the other five four-year-olds to the public playground, which happens to be adjacent to one of Albany's new magnet schools. While the six classmates were happily playing together on one of the climbing structures, a group of slightly older kids from the magnet school sidled over and began teasing the only boy in Mumasatou's group, who was quite small for his age. Abe was obviously intimidated, but continued playing with his group, trying hard to ignore his tormentors, who smelled blood and slowly began moving in for the kill. As I sat watching this drama unfold from a discreet distance, debating whether or not to intervene on Abe's behalf, the next thing I knew Mumasatou had placed herself directly between Abe and the other boys. Just like some ancient tai chi master, she pretended at first not to notice that anything was going on, and instead continued to jabber with Abe and her girlfriends. Those foolish boys, unimpressed by her presence, continued their teasing; the next thing I overheard was Mumasatou telling them they shouldn't be saying the things they were saying. This brought their attention squarely onto her, which of course was what she had in mind in the first place. Now came time for the hapless bullies' big mistake. They began calling her "stupid girl" and other less printable names.

Just like in the old martial arts flicks, it was over in a flash. All Mumasatou had to do was give them one of her patented looks and issue a single threat, one that any Marine drill sergeant would have been proud to have uttered, and those boys, gaining in wisdom rapidly, were sent running for their lives. Mumasatou chased them for a hundred yards or so and then nonchalantly returned to her perch and picked up right where she had left off.

Thus the same little girl who could be so stubbornly selfish and domineering could also be the best friend you'd ever want to have. Her loyalty and caring were equal to her rage. And while it was always a case of two steps forward and one step back, by the end of her second year with us, her violent outbursts had greatly diminished in frequency and duration, and her ability to handle frustration had grown by leaps and bounds.

MUMASATOU, THROUGH HER uninhibited displays of aggression, was instructing us daily that it is imperative for anyone who works closely with children to have some deeper understanding of the twin phenomena of power and aggression.

Mind you, this may not be as easy as it sounds. As George Bach stated in another important book from the 1970s, *Creative Aggression,* modern middle-class American society has begun to hold aggression as one of its primary taboos. This generalized prohibition is now giving rise to an entire generation whose first impulse is to avoid conflict and aggression, manifesting instead all sorts of hidden or indirect ways of expressing anger and hostility, and thereby wreaking untold havoc on intimate relationships everywhere.

Children like Mumasatou are crying out to be reckoned with by emotionally aware adults who can meet their youthful displays of power with just the right level of response. They need to be met not with punishment or its opposite, permissiveness, but with compassion and truthful directness. In other words, they need adults who have come to terms with their own innate aggression and who know when they should intervene and when it's okay to let them thrash things out on their own terms. But, if conflicts are to be allowed to take their natural course—as is so often the case at the Free School—then it is imperative that the teachers be sensitively attuned to the various levels of each individual situation, paying special attention to the interior states of the children involved. Those adults must have contact with the full range of human emotions so that they can sense when a child is just out to dump anger and inflict injury, in which case they must be able to respond quickly, creatively, and effectively.

I recently observed a situation in which the adults involved clearly didn't have a clue: We had taken the preschoolers to the same aforementioned playground, when a fight suddenly broke out between two girls from the nearby magnet school who looked about ten or eleven. Incredible as it may seem, the three teachers attending this class of about fifteen kids were unable to stop the fight. While they stood passively by looking worried and uncertain, the situation quickly developed into a real-life *Lord of the Flies* scene. The other kids crowded closer and closer around the two enraged girls, taunting them and egging them on. Several of the boys started darting into the circle and attacking one of the girls, who was on the verge of obesity and was clearly the group outcast. Still, nothing the three teachers did to try to halt this increasingly ugly scene had any effect. I had already left our group and was about to intervene myself when the adults finally managed to herd their angry swarm back into the building, the kids' fists flying all the while.

Unable to see how the disturbance ended, I returned to where our kids were busily playing and began to reflect on what had happened. It was sad to see a group of human beings demonstrating such a complete lack of ability to work through a conflict. I suspect aggression is thoroughly prohibited during their school day, so that when it inevitably breaks out it becomes something for the entire class to get off on. Certainly this was one of the themes of William Golding's novel. Meanwhile, the teachers miss out on any opportunity to gain experience in conflict resolution. Although I didn't get to see the conclusion to this playground fracas, my guess is that once the class was back inside the school building, the two combatants were separated from the rest and penalties were assessed privately according to some predetermined policy. Thus the entire group, teachers as well as students, was denied any true closure.

The issue of aggression is a tricky one because there are so few generalizations that hold up very well. Every child is unique; every situation different. Some kids, for example, are too passive or adaptive, and actually need help loosening up their emotional controls. These are the kids we often tend to worry about because they seem to lack the inner permission to assert themselves and instead are too willing to put up with unsatisfactory situations—an unlikely outcome for Mumasatou. So often, they are the ones who are destined for some later form of unfulfillment, convinced that they were victims of their circumstances. In plain language, what they need are opportunities as children to learn to stick up for themselves.

Now this is by no means the same as learning to fight. We are well aware of the many risks involved in permitting kids to engage in conflicts according to their own rules, and so over the years we have come up with numerous tools for both the prevention and resolution of personal violence.

For example, in order to foster prevention we borrowed the "stop rule" from Jerry Mintz's Shaker Mountain School in Burlington, Vermont. It is very simple and serves as a perfect complement to our council meeting system. The way it works is this: Whenever anyone is being treated in an unacceptable manner—teased, threatened, shoved around, bullied—all he or she has to do is yell "STOP" in a good, clear voice. If the offender doesn't discontinue his or her actions immediately, then the offended party has the option of calling a council meeting.

The mechanics of a council meeting, where many a future conflict is prevented and many a current one resolved, are as follows: Anybody can call a meeting at any time. By general agreement (also subject to change at any time—a six-year-old once got the mandatory-attendance-at-council-meetings clause voted out temporarily), when a meeting is called, we all drop what we are doing and go to the largest room on the first floor of the building, where we sit in a large circle on the carpet. Three nominations are forwarded and a chairperson is elected (usually a student, sometimes as young as six). It is the chair's responsibility to recognize speakers, keep the discussion on track, and maintain order. Interestingly, while the atmosphere of the school is characteristically freewheeling, strict decorum is required in council meetings at all times—and everyone takes them very seriously.

The general rule of thumb is that meetings are called only for urgent matters, and only after other alternatives have been exhausted. The chair begins by asking whoever called the meeting to state his or her problem. If the matter is deemed trivial by the group, the meeting is usually quickly adjourned; in cases where someone has repeatedly "cried wolf," a motion might be passed prohibiting that individual from calling any more meetings for a prescribed length of time (which sometimes sets off wonderful constitutional debates). All meetings are run in accordance with *Robert's Rules of Order*, and policies are made and changed, consequences meted out, and so on, by majority vote. When the issue is a particularly serious one, the discussion tends to continue until some sort of consensus is reached, but this is not required. A meeting generally concludes when the person who called it considers the problem solved and makes a motion to adjourn. Not every meeting has a happy ending, and it sometimes takes several go-arounds before a genuine resolution is achieved.

The council meeting structure serves a number of important functions in the day-to-day life of the school, but its real genius is the way it keeps aggression from turning into a toxic force. Since it gives even the smallest kids power equal to or greater than the oldest and largest—via strength in numbers—bullying and gangstering are easily controlled. Violations of the stop rule are always taken very seriously by the other kids.

The therapeutic potential of council meetings is practically limitless. With the need for personal privacy and confidentiality respected at all times, meetings become a safe, supportive space where the origins of problems can be examined. Maybe the conflict started with something that happened a day or two before at school, or with some kind of trouble at home (an abusive older sibling, parents fighting, etc.). Tears are not infrequent.

One might wonder how there can be such a high degree of internal harmony in an environment with so few outwardly visible rules and regulations. The answer, I think, lies in the inherent logic of the council meeting system. Important issues rarely go unaddressed for long; furthermore, a level of trust and an accompanying sense of community are established, which in and of themselves are a natural deterrent to the kinds of aggressive behavior most schools work so hard to rule out of existence.

Here are the shortcomings I see in conventional school approaches to aggression. Relying on external rules and punishments to keep the peace seldom accomplishes this goal because children who habitually act out their anger tend to respond in one of two ways: either they continue to escalate their aggressive behavior until they get themselves thrown out (or nowadays drugged out of their feelings), or they go underground with their anger and become human versions of a ticking time bomb. What these kids need, instead, is to discover for themselves that they have a problem that is costing *them* something—not just punishment or loss of privileges, but loss of friendship, of their standing in the community, and of feeling good about themselves. They are far more likely to take in this kind of information from their peers.

Second, when interpersonal conflicts are always settled in a tidy, adult-managed way, the child-antagonists are denied the chance to develop their own unique ways of handling themselves in conflict situations, and perhaps most important of all, to invent solutions that work.

Since the Free School has no standardized responses to out-of-bounds behavior, kids have an opportunity to gain important self-knowledge based on the trials and tribulations of their own experience. Of course, it goes without saying that this kind of thing would be impossible in the large, centralized schools that have become the modern norm. Paul Goodman wrote way back in the 1960s about the need for large cities like his native New York to have a school on every block so that problems would have manageable dimensions and real community could be embraced.

NOW FIVE GOING on fifteen, Mumasatou would bless us with one more year of her trying, gift-filled presence. In many ways she was now a different child; in many ways still the same. Thankfully, she seemed to be well on her way to discovering that she could get nurturing without having to fight for it and without it coming at anyone else's expense. As her repertoire for getting positive attention steadily expanded, we saw correspondingly fewer of the negative behaviors of the previous years.

But there remained one area where there was little, if any, change. Whenever a teacher would attempt to lead any kind of group activity that included her, especially if it was at all frustration-provoking, Mumasatou usually regressed in a hurry, virtually guaranteeing her a monopoly on the adult attention she so coveted. For instance, she loved being read to, and was beginning to learn certain favorite stories by heart, but she was rarely willing to sit and listen in a group. The same was true with art projects and with any kind of skills-oriented lesson. Forced to share the teacher with even one other child, she would quickly become overwhelmed with jealousy and dream up one reason or another to come apart at the seams.

I will never forget the day Richard, who was divorced and had been living alone in the community, invited his beautiful new girlfriend to have lunch with him at the school. Within minutes Mumasatou had managed to worm herself and her untouched plate between the two lovebirds. Next, she slowly worked her way onto Richard's lap, all the while shooting hard stares at his friend. Of course she insisted on eating off of his plate, continuing to ignore her own. Finally came the kicker: "Oooh Richie, are you goin' to fuck her?" she asked, grinning wickedly from ear to ear. At that point I came to the rescue so that the two totally nonplussed diners could at least finish eating. After Richard's friend left, he had one helluva time extricating himself from Mumasatou's clutches. "Please don't go, Richie. Pleeeease." He and his girlfriend tended to meet elsewhere after that.

It was this year that Mumasatou began showing an occasional interest in participating in the kindergarten, which generally meets separately for an hour or two each day in one semi-walled-off corner of the Big Room to work on projects and activities for developing basic reading, writing, and arithmetic skills. The older preschoolers join in when they are ready and start asking to participate. Mumasatou would sometimes choose to come in and sometimes not, depending on her mood.

Luckily, Deb was the teacher. She was a real old pro with kids this age, especially girls. She was also a calm, easygoing soul and—a folk music performer after hours—in possession of a wonderfully soothing voice. But try as Deb might to avert Mumasatou's fits of jealousy, there were often six or eight other kids in the room also needing attention, and Mumasatou's early exits grew almost predictable. Having another adult present to assist Deb helped somewhat, but nothing short of constant one-on-one attention would suffice if Mumasatou began experiencing even the slightest frustration.

Not unexpectedly, Mumasatou's mother started asking about her child's progress and if she would be ready for first grade the next year. We lose a lot of kids between five and six, especially from inner-city families. The cultural ethic—no doubt an artifact of universal compulsory education—that says that at six "it's time to get to work" is a powerful one, and hard to get many parents to look at differently. They're worried their kids will grow lazy and spoiled and then "fall behind." Also, first grade in public school doesn't cost anything. Even though we ask families to pay only what they can afford, some prefer to take the society up on its offer of free primary education.

If Mumasatou were indeed headed for public school, I wasn't too excited about her chances—a fact I tried several times to get across to her mother. Given that she had difficulty sharing her teacher with a handful of other students where participation was voluntary, how would she ever manage in a classroom with thirty kids and the virtual absence of choice?

Even though Mumasatou's mother wasn't settled about the following year, we decided we'd better do what we could to help prepare Mumasatou to make the transition to public school if it did occur. For a brief period during the middle of the school year, Deb even tried insisting that she come into the kindergarten room every morning, leaving her free to do whatever she wanted once she was there. The strategy worked pretty well at first. Mumasatou would come in with the others of her own accord, and Deb then made a point of initiating projects involving a lot of excitement and creativity. More often than not, Mumasatou's curiosity would get the better of her and she would join in, thoroughly enjoying herself in the process. On other days, she would remain separate from the rest of the group, absorbed in her own activities, which was fine, or she would participate from a distance, which was fine, too.

Unfortunately, after awhile the novelty wore off and Mumasatou began refusing to attend the class at all. Deb continued to insist gently, but to no one's surprise, forcing the child's compliance proved to be totally counterproductive. As kids so often do in this type of situation, Mumasatou began applying her abundant genius and creativity toward inventing newer and better ways of disruption. Not wanting to reinforce the old behaviors we had worked so hard to help her grow out of, Deb immediately returned to the old system, where Mumasatou only attended kindergarten when she felt like it.

"THE SCHOOL MUST fit the student and not the other way around," wrote A. S. Neill in *Summerhill*. In our case, Mumasatou's absolute refusal to fit into our customary patterns had put us to the test once more. Should we escalate our efforts to get her to conform or should we again allow her the space to learn and grow in her own idiosyncratic, willful way?

We could have cited her "inability" to focus, her "short attention span," her lack of demonstrable progress in reading and writing, her high energy level, her uncooperativeness, and her impulsive, aggressive behavior. Then we could have directed her mother to have her "tested" by an educational "psychologist" whose professional task it would be to ascribe to her one sort of pathological label or another. Most likely he would have selected attention deficit disorder, probably with an h thrown in for "hyperactivity." All of this, of course, adds up to ADHD—the latest designer tag for kids like Mumasatou who insist on defying the society's demand that they stay in lockstep with a set of preordained standards.

But we didn't do any of those things. Instead, we chose to recognize that Mumasatou's developmental track was as unique as she was. And, more important, we honored her right to say no. Having let her into our hearts—as she had done so totally with us—we understood implicitly that Mumasatou was simply not an adaptive type. She wouldn't have been able to survive in the world of her origin if she had been. We knew her refusal to do the things the other kids in her group were doing didn't mean there was anything wrong with her. It was obvious to us that she was un*willing*, not un*able*, to do them. Or perhaps she just wasn't ready.

There was certainly nothing wrong with her attention span. Day after day she spent hours on end concentratedly working with clay or playing with dolls. And who's to say that her activity level was too high—that she was *hyper*active? In other words, we knew that her independent, energetic ways were not a sign that she had a *disorder* of some kind. I believe the same to be true of so many of the children being negatively judged by our modern, "scientific" methods of assessment. Their offense is not ignorance or substandard performance, it is willful individuality and nonconformity—which I was taught in high school is only a crime in totalitarian societies.

Furthermore, if we had compelled Mumasatou to be and do things that she was either unready for or simply uninterested in at a given moment, we probably would have missed out on most, if not all, of her positive and noble qualities. Isn't the truth of the matter that all children carry within them their own particular form of genius? And isn't it incumbent upon schools and the teachers and administrators who comprise them, as A. S. Neill insisted, to adapt to the needs of their students so as to elicit that genius? My answer to these questions incorporates something every good teacher, I think, takes for granted: namely, how important it is to build on children's strengths rather than dwell on—and penalize them for—their apparent weaknesses.

In the realm of medicine we now know that sometimes the procedures or medications doctors employ in treating their patients can themselves become the cause of distress. We have even come up with a term for this phenomenon: iatrogenic illness. Perhaps it is time to coin a similar term to describe what happens when schools create problem children by treating them mechanistically, as though they were uniformly square pegs supposed to fit through equally uniform round holes. What is it that keeps us from recognizing that the way schools treat children is so very often the cause of the supposed symptoms? This question I will leave to others, and conclude simply by saying that had we demanded of Mumasatou that *she* conform to *our* regimen, *we* would have been the problem.

At the Free School we try not to adhere too religiously to any one particular approach, preferring instead to go with whatever works. Some children need absolute hands off so that they can begin finding their own way, while others, if they are holding back out of fear or lack of confidence, need encouragement and guidance and maybe even a gentle push or two. This didn't work in Mumasatou's case.

What she did need from us was patience and tolerance for her distinctive personality and her personal developmental timetable, not some bizarre Orwellian label affixed to her permanent record. That cowardly practice is only another way of blaming the victim. Professionals who engage in such labeling should have heavy stones hung around their necks so that they can begin to get a feel for what they have done to already vulnerable children in declaring with all of the formidable weight of their position that they suffer from some sort of pathological condition. What damnable nonsense.

MUMASATOU WASN'T SPENDING time in the kindergarten with her peers, but she wasn't sitting around eating chocolates and watching soap operas either. She wasn't lazy and she wasn't exploiting the freedom of choice that she enjoyed. Quite to the contrary, she was learning all the time. And she was busy being a valuable and valued member of the larger school community.

For instance, that year we had taken on a two-year-old bilingual French-speaking boy who was suffering from separation anxiety while he was in school each day. Mumasatou, perhaps better than anyone else, understood his deep sense of abandonment. In return, he trusted her implicitly. And, unpredictable though she might be, we trusted her with him.

When Miles was having one of his bad days, Mumasatou became his at-school mother. They would spend hours together happily amusing one another. She would read to him, sing to him, dress him up, comfort him when he cried, and when the weather was nice, take him out back and push him on the swings or play with him in the sandbox. Here was a role she was well-versed in—mothering—and while she was playing it, she was making an important contribution, one for which we made sure to recognize her. I'm not certain Miles could have managed without her during his first tentative months in school.

Mumasatou contributed in other important ways as well. You might say she was our school psychologist. Thanks to her uncanny intuitive ability, she usually knew exactly what was going on with other people—who meant what they said and who didn't, who was harboring racist attitudes and who wasn't—and she would tailor her treatment to each particular case. I finally realized one day that the individuals I would see her hanging all over and endlessly pestering—age being no factor—were, in fact, depressed. Mumasatou, playing therapist, was trying to get them to snap out of it! She had a way of pushing overly passive people—kids or adults—until they pushed back with effectiveness.

Mumasatou, in other words, possessed the same deep knowing that one can find in a great many little kids if one knows how to observe and talk to them. By insisting on testing and retesting her reality every day, she was well on her way to a very grown-up understanding of such fundamental principles as truth, respect, personal power, and responsibility. The Free School never presumed that its role was to "teach" her these lessons. Rather we considered it our job to maintain for her an environment where she could safely work them out for herself. Only in this way might she discover that her life belonged to her.

How well we succeeded remains to be seen. Toward the end of the school year, Mumasatou began making stronger and stronger statements that next year she wanted to switch to the beleaguered elementary school not far from her home, where her older sisters and brothers went. Much as we didn't feel that she was ready, we told her to talk it over with her mother; if it was okay with her, we would "graduate" her in June.

One thing we have learned over the years is not to try to keep kids in our school after they have gotten the idea that it is time for them to move on. This is a decision that different children or their families make at different points for very different reasons. Tiffany, mentioned earlier, chose to leave us when she was only seven—over her parents' loud protests—so that she could go to her small-town school, where all her friends went.

The Free School's magic only works because we hold no hostages. All who are present in the building at any given time are there because they want to be, not because they have to be. And we have found again and again that when it has, in fact, been the child's choice to leave, he or she tends to manage fine with the ensuing transition. It is as though the act of making their own authentic choice about where they will go to school in and of itself propels them forward.

Not surprisingly, convince her mother she did; although whether the decision to leave was Mumasatou's decision or really her mother's we'll never know. Her pals Ashley and Tiara would also be moving on to public school in September, which meant that at least she would be in good company. I had very much hoped she would remain with us until she was more confident in a group context and further along in acquiring her basic skills; but then, as was so often the case, she had other ideas.

AGAIN AND AGAIN, outside observers have told us that they see a noticeable difference in Free School kids. We once had an intern come over from Japan, an excellent teacher with more than ten years' experience back home. I'll always remember how, upon his arrival, he observed with spontaneous amazement: "Your students all have such shiny eyes!" He went on to say that in his many years of working with children, he had never seen such a display of aliveness.

Mumasatou would leave us with as much as she was taking away. She had helped to teach us that it is possible to help children grow and thrive— within appropriate limits and safe boundaries—without robbing them of any of the rich exuberance that is their birthright. I am quite certain that her transformation would never have occurred unless we had been willing to trust in the unpredictable freedom dance that plays itself out in the Free School every day.

3

Fixing a Desk, Mending a Mind

'Tis a gift to be simple,
'Tis a gift to be free
'Tis a gift to come down
Where we ought to be.

—from an old Shaker hymn

Hands to work,
Hearts to God.

—Shaker motto

We're grateful when difficult children like Mumasatou come to us at an early age. They are so much more innocent then, so much less set in their ways. Perhaps this, above all, is why we instituted a preschool program in the first place. A great many don't find us until they're already in a big mess—like Jesse, who came at the age of twelve with a long history of school troubles, both academic and behavioral.

Big for his age, foulmouthed and prone to harassing smaller kids, Jesse, thankfully, was not a tough kid. There was a certain physical softness about him that could also be found on the inside, beneath the veneer of jive talk and intimidation—somewhere in the region of the heart. In other words, the "Yo, don't mess with me!" posturing was just that: a protective mask covering layers of raw, untreated wounds that extended a long way back, maybe even into the womb.

Loss had been Jesse's constant companion. His mother—now fully recovered—was virtually lost to drug addiction for much of his early childhood. His older brother died when Jesse was seven; his father not long after that. His favorite uncle, very much a godfather figure, died while Jesse was in our school.

What happens to a child who has a lifetime of loss packed into a single, abbreviated childhood? The answer, of course, is never a simple one. The outcome—whether that boy or girl survives intact or is swallowed up by the same life-denying patterns of existence passed down from previous generations—will be determined by many factors, some originating inside, some coming from outside of the child's home. In Jesse's case, thanks in large part to a gutsy mother who managed to face her demons and reclaim her life and family, and to a new stepfather who is on a similar path, he had not hardened against his pain, and therein lay the source of his salvation. Thankfully, too, Jesse's mother noticed that her son was falling between the cracks, and she was able to search out the right alternative for him before it was too late.

What this deep wounding does to virtually all children, I think, regardless of their circumstances, is to lay them wide open to the influence of the worst aspects of the popular culture. This was obvious with Jesse. When I actually listened to what he was saying when he was running his mouth, I realized the words came straight from the latest gangsta rap hit. His presenting attitudes and mannerisms were right off the street corner. Once, he even showed up with an old, worn-out beeper on his belt. When he realized that no one was the least bit impressed, it disappeared just as suddenly as it had appeared.

Meanwhile, most of the time the real Jesse was hiding just out of sight, very easy to spot if only you knew where to look. He appeared at first glance to be a stereotypically "hyperactive" kid—impulsive, aggressive, short attention span, the whole nine yards. But when I observed him even for just a moment or two when he was tired (fortunately, his battery did run down from time to time), I could easily see the depression, the grief, the pain, the fear, the anger, and the disappointment from which his hyperactivity serves to distract him—and others. As is the case with any good magician, three-quarters of Jesse's act was simply a diversion to lure the eyes away from what is really going on.

None of this is to say that Jesse was a dishonest child; in fact, when push came to shove he was perhaps the most honest person in his class.

Though he didn't quite realize it yet, his pain had been his teacher for a long time. It had deepened him and given him thoughts about things of which most kids have only scratched the surface. The other kids appreciated this about Jesse and it helped them to tolerate his all-too-frequent bouts of obnoxiousness.

The repair work to Jesse's heart began the day he entered our school. Actually, it probably began the day Jesse's mother decided to take hold of her life again, but I can only relate here the part I was around to witness. It began when we told him that he was free to do as he pleased in school, as long as he was respectful and didn't violate the rights or sensibilities of others. It began when we told his parents that he might go an entire year without doing any apparent schoolwork, but asked them not to worry because he was a perfectly intelligent and capable child who would be more than able to catch up academically as soon as *he* chose to invest himself in the process. And it began with Jesse coming to school every day because he *wanted* to and not because he *had* to.

Even today, after all these years, I sometimes find myself stopping to wonder how we could possibly tell a boy who was a certified failure by conventional school standards and who was years behind academically (again by conventional school standards) that he didn't have to do any schoolwork. And where do we find the hutzpah to ask his parents not to worry about the academic progress of a twelve-year-old whom they have been told for years is headed for disaster? Always, the quicker I respond to these outbreaks of profound doubt the better; and every time, the answer to the question is the same: *the heart will lead the head every time.*

We began by simply setting Jesse free: free from the pressure of an academic timetable and its endless performance assessments, from constant behavioral monitoring and adult intervention, and perhaps even more important, free to think his own thoughts, to choose his own activities, and to associate freely with a wide range of other children—not just alleged problem ones like himself.

Jesse's bullying was not much of an issue initially because there were two older boys in the school who took it upon themselves to keep him in check. The following year was another story, however. Then Jesse was the senior boy, and sure enough, he immediately set out in September to take full advantage of his physical supremacy by lording it over the smaller kids. This state of affairs persisted until a coalition of them banded together in a council meeting and figured out a way to bell the cat. The meeting had courageously been called by Zach, one of the next younger boys, who after grilling Jesse with a series of "Why do you always do this?" and "Why do you always do that?" questions, made a motion that Jesse would have to pay a five-dollar fine the next time he intimidated a smaller student. It passed with only one dissenting vote (guess whose), and needless to say there was no next time. Jesse looked relieved after that.

WILHELM REICH ONCE said that a bent tree will never grow straight. Of course, as a depth psychologist Reich was using this metaphor to emphasize the importance of preventing damage to children's psyches from occurring in the first place.

Today the picture is, if anything, bleaker than it was in Reich's tumultuous day. Jesse's story is a common one now. Due to myriad causes, the society is busy producing entire forests of bent trees. Our major cities have become dangerous places to live and their schools hostility-breeding holding pens. We continue to witness the failure of one socially engineered masssolution after another. Boilerplate school reform initiatives and pilot projects tend to work only for a brief time and then to help only a fortunate few.

It's true that bent trees never grow straight; however, they can compensate for adverse conditions in the most amazing ways, provided they aren't stressed to the point of disease or death. The trees in my large, inner-city backyard are an excellent example: shaded by much taller trees left to grow wild in a neighboring lot, they managed to reach the sunlight they need by growing sideways for awhile at a rather steep angle until they could once again extend upward to the open sky. In the meantime, we tended and mulched and fertilized them, so that today they are beautiful and healthy specimens, if a bit unusual looking.

And so it is with children, who often possess unfathomable resilience and the ability to adapt unless they are pushed beyond human limits. We can help them grow straighter—one at a time.

But how? In Jesse's case, did we expect to change him simply by blanketing him with love and understanding, freeing up enough open space for him to grow into, and then looking the other way when he chose to unload his pain on another, usually smaller child? Hardly, but on the other hand, we now know from long experience that stepping up the "discipline" and increasing the supervision and external motivation—the standard response of most schools to nonconforming students—is so often simply a setup for some form of permanent failure, or at best, a way of disguising or delaying it.

No, the medicine we administered to Jesse might best be called *the truth*. When he was behaving like a moron, someone would tell him— straight and to his face. And when he acted courageously or insightfully, the same was true. When his jokes were funny, people laughed at them; when they weren't, they didn't. And when his language or behavior exceeded acceptable limits, someone—not necessarily the teachers—would stop him in his tracks. As the saying used to go, we were "real" with Jesse at all times, and he grew to count on that. And suddenly he found himself with the space he had never had before to experiment with new behaviors and to fashion new expectations.

WE BEGAN SEEING sometimes dramatic improvements in Jesse's overall attitude and demeanor, but not in his academic prowess. Though his ability to stay with activities that excited him—gymnastics and the computer being his favorites—increased steadily over time, his resistance to any kind of organized academic study remained massive as he entered his second half-year with us. He would occasionally join in on a class in history, math, or science, but always with the same result: he would quickly lose interest and then, like Mumasatou, resort to his old dysfunctional, attention-grabbing behaviors, which would earn him the same negative reward as in his former schools— the teacher would send him packing. The only difference here is that we don't attach any additional meaning to this outcome. Jesse wasn't punished for his transgression and where he went after he was asked to leave a class was his business (there's no principal's office at the Free School). He was always welcome to come back as soon as he was ready to make the same commitment as the others. In other words, attending classes in our school isn't an obligation, it's a privilege.

Our older students usually spend at least part of each week involved in an apprenticeship or internship in an area of strong interest to them. Over the years they have worked with veterinarians, lawyers, artists, writers, dancers, models, cartoonists, magicians, boat builders, photographers, horse trainers, pilots, museum curators, chefs, and computer engineers. Again, no obligation; though almost everyone jumps at the chance to be around an adult who's doing something they think they might like to try one day. Thankfully, there never seems to be a shortage of willing adults.

This year Jesse had asked to work with Frank, a member of the Free School community. Frank is a craftsman in his sixties who co-owns a small, independent woodworking shop specializing in traditional wooden boats and cars. Since Frank's shop is next door to the school, Jesse and Frank already had a passing acquaintance, and I suspect that Jesse was at least as drawn to the person of Frank—the father of five grown sons—as he was to the kind of work that Frank does. This is one very valuable aspect of the apprenticeship model of education: it restores the teaching/learning exchange to where it rightfully belongs, embedded in the relationship between two people.

Jesse had been spending one morning a week with Frank in his shop, watching and helping him while he worked on his cars and his boats, as well as doing the chores that all apprentices in woodshops do—sweeping, fetching and putting away tools, stacking wood, and whatnot. When the time came for Jesse to begin work on a project of his own, which he would be asked to display to parents, students, and teachers on Apprenticeship Night at the school, serendipity struck again.

It just so happened that Jesse had a rather unique relationship with his school desk, which was one of a wide assortment of hand-me-downs from inner-city public schools that had closed their doors to children long ago. They span several generations of design style, from old oak ones with beautiful bent-wood braces to modern Formica models with legs of tubular steel. Jesse, of course, had managed to lay claim to one of the really nice, old wooden ones.

To Jesse a school desk was anything but a place to do schoolwork. He used his more like a nightstand, or a coffee table perhaps, a place to stack things carelessly—tape players and tapes, portable video games, sweaters, coats, hats, and gloves. And on the rare occasions when the top of the desk happened to be uncluttered, it served as a decreasingly sturdy, elevated seat.

Over the years I have observed something about schoolbooks that I think applies equally well to Jesse's desk. I can tell when a child is having difficulty with arithmetic, or just plain doesn't like the subject, by the appearance (or disappearance) of his or her workbook. If he or she does manage to hang on to it, it quickly begins to look like something that got stuck in a department store escalator, with the cover torn and dog-eared and numerous pages missing. Since Jesse had yet to choose to have any books of his own, it was his desk that became the concrete symbol of his years of frustration and failure in school. He carved it, he scribbled on it, he rocked it, he kicked it, he knocked it over; finally one day he sat on it with a little too much gusto and it collapsed into a heap of its composite pieces, with him on top.

What did I do when I saw the mess? Did I scold him for destroying school property? Or lecture him about the proper use of school desks? Actually, I laughed out loud, amused by the fact that in all my years of teaching, I had never before seen anyone manage to reduce a desk to rubble. Then, remembering that he had an apprenticeship at the boat shop, I asked him if he would be willing to ask Frank to help him restore the desk. Jesse thought for a moment or two and said that he would at their next session.

Jesse's relationship with Frank (and vice versa) had been coming along quite nicely, so Frank was more than glad to help Jesse with his desk. It would be lovely at this point to present a tidy and orderly picture of Jesse's progress in his apprenticeship. The trouble is that learning, growth, and change usually don't happen in a systematic way. They occur in fits and starts, the result of the timely interplay between forces of outward momentum and inward inertia.

Here are excerpts from the journal I asked Frank to keep, which illustrate what I mean:

> Jesse wants to be in the shop with us. He's interested enough to watch while I work. Every chance I get, I teach names of tools, measuring, design and layout, business, and so on. Whatever is up is what is being taught. The tests are: "Jesse, please bring me the sliding square," or "Measure the length and width of that board for me."

> He's willing to write! Does a better than average job with his journal. That's a hopeful sign in a lad who's been branded a school failure. I've told him daily journaling is a requirement of this apprenticeship; he not only does it, I think he's actually in accord with it.

> Jesse says he's terrible at math. As we work with measurement, design, and layout I find that, yes, he's lacking. His basic skills are sound, though, and little by little he lets on that he knows more than he was willing to show initially. There's skill there for the developing, when he wants it.

> Jesse's school desk is broken (later I learn he tore it apart himself) and he asks if he can bring it to the shop and fix it. Sounds like a good project to me, but my work time is precious, so I ask if we can work on it during lunch hours. He agrees happily and brings in a sad pile of desk parts.

> I told Jesse to come in for his regular apprentice time and then at noon we will grab a quick bite and work on the desk. He doesn't show at the appointed time and I assume he's out of school. I make an appointment with a customer for noon, and then, just as I'm going out the door, Jesse shows. I can't change things again so I tell him we'll do it Thursday and make sure he understands the timing. I can see he's disappointed. There seems to be some mistrust there, too.

> Thursday, Jesse shows on schedule and helps with work on a wooden car body. At noon we rush next door, grab a bite, and head back to the shop. We start taking the remainder of the desk apart and cleaning the joints for regluing. I'm teaching as we work, and Jesse, motivation high, is chugging right along with me. At one point he remarks on a loose leg joint and asks how to fix it. I tell him that the only way that really works well is to take it apart, clean it, and reglue it. I say that this particular joint will be OK when the rest of the desk is assembled around it, though, so don't bother. But he is curious about how one takes apart such a joint and we discuss it, then I get distracted by a phone call. A couple of minutes later I hear Jesse say,

"Shit!" He has broken the joint while trying to get it apart. Didn't want any half-measures in rehabbing his desk. I'm annoyed at him and he hears it in my voice. Then I say, "It's OK, Jess. It can be fixed." So we discuss how to heal the break. Ten minutes later I see him holding the offending part and muttering with a dark look on his face. I ask, "Mad at yourself, Jesse?" He admits it and then I tell him, "Hey, what we've done here is create an opportunity to learn!" I go on to tell him how many times in my life I've created similar opportunities for myself. He gets it and starts to smile. I am reminded why I take on an apprentice every now and then.

Apprenticeship Night is coming up and Jesse seems in a quandary about what to do. I don't think the desk will be finished by then. I get the feeling that this is a familiar scenario for him. Another incompletion. Another failure to finish. I say, "Lets get some photos of the pieces and what you're doing to them. I think those, along with whatever you've got done on the desk and your journal will make a good exhibit." Again the smile and I sense relief. . . . "I'm gonna finish this time!"

We take the photos and glue up the desk. Tune in tomorrow. . . .

The beauty of the apprenticeship model is that it kills so many birds with one stone. For starters, it gives kids the message that the adult world is worth learning about. Then it provides the perfect environment for that learning: the workplace. It also supplies the framework within which a nurturing relationship can develop between mentor and apprentice. Finally, it gives the student a respite from the constant supervision and performance monitoring upon which most schools depend so heavily. Apprenticeship enables schools to communicate a very important message to their rapidly maturing students: we recognize that you are grown up enough now to work and learn independently and derive your own value from your own experience.

Additionally, of course, apprenticeships give kids a chance to explore future career possibilities with great immediacy, and often lead, either directly or indirectly, to both current and future job opportunities. And, of course, you can't beat the economics—labor in exchange for teaching.

Frank's journal clearly reveals how mutually beneficial the arrangement was. We can readily see the deepening, multilevel relationship between mentor and apprentice, one that would be far less likely ever to occur between teacher and student in a standard classroom, due to all of the excess baggage carried by that authority-bound dynamic. And this applies even to our school. I could tell that Jesse was sweating bullets over Apprenticeship Night. But, as the time approached and he began presenting to me excuse after excuse for why he wouldn't be able to attend, all I could do as his teacher was to set the limits for him by telling him if he didn't show up I would have his hide. It was Frank—as mentor—who was able to help Jesse through the barriers of his own resistance.

ACCOMPANIED BY FRANK, Jesse not only made it to Apprenticeship Night, he glowed as he showed off his partially completed project and answered question after question about how on earth he was able to put that helter-skelter collection of parts shown in the photos back into such a strong and stable four-legged structure. And on that evening, Jesse declared his intention not only to reconstruct the desk, but to refinish it as well. It was then that I realized I couldn't wait to see him seated either at or on that freshly varnished, gleaming antique, because at that moment he would have—perhaps for the first time in his young life—an entirely legitimate basis for lording it over his peers.

Along with that image came the realization that Jesse, now thirteen, was not only learning how to repair broken furniture, he was taking all of the necessary steps for mending a damaged mind. And wasn't it perfect that the piece Jesse had chosen to invest so many hours of effort in was an old public school desk, one at which countless children had sat over the years, some no doubt suffering through the same negativity he had endured until now.

4

The Therapeutic School

Wise hearts find truth in paradox.

—from a Protestant hymn

There's no doubt about it; we are different from most other schools. For instance, whenever we encounter other nursery school or day care center groups in the neighborhood, I'm always struck by the orderliness of the children as they pad passively along, two by two. Knowing ours the way I do, it's hard to imagine how their kids could be so compliant, until one of them takes a step out of line and you discover that their every move is being monitored by a nearby adult ready with a reprimand.

Don't get me wrong here—I'm not advocating that little kids be allowed to run out into the street in order to learn about traffic. It's just that, in general, we seem to give our kids a lot more room to roam. Whenever we head off to the park, the scene resembles the start of the Indianapolis 500, a dozen or more kids screeching off the starting line and zooming up to the next street corner, where they wait for the slowpokes to catch up. To insure safety we simply tell the kids in no uncertain terms that anyone who cannot be counted on to stay out of the street will have to hold a teacher's hand until such time as they can be trusted. Ninety-nine times out of a hundred, that's all it takes.

Meanwhile, since we routinely accept kids like Mumasatou and Jesse, and since we appear as such a motley crew—teachers

47

included—someone is always asking if we are some kind of special school, for (you know) "special" (problem) children. Of course, I always want to answer, "Yes!" because damn it, all children are special, and all children have problems. We all have problems for that matter; it's the nature of the beast.

Actually, we are not a school that is specially designed for anyone. Year after year we simply try to take on whoever happens to show up. And since we are just about the only affordable alternative to the conventional school model in a metropolitan region with more than a quarter of a million people, where the only entrance requirement is a genuine desire to be a full participant in the life of the school, you can count on some very interesting characters appearing every year.

Roughly, I would say that we are a "school of last resort" for about a third of our fifty students, who range in age from two to fourteen. Another third seek us out because they and their parents are attracted to our unorthodox approach to education, with the remaining third coming because we are simply their neighborhood school. This last group struggles mightily to come to terms with our unusual style, and we try to help them bridge the gap as much as possible.

We consider ourselves to be a "therapeutic school." Mary says the Free School is like a Rorschach test, meaning that whatever someone experiences in our school is simply an outward manifestation of the inner rumblings of that person's psyche. In other words, if one has preconceived ideas about school, or about life in general, then sooner or later one will get reality to bear that out. For this reason, we always tell prospective parents that if their kids are coming to us because of problems in a previous school, they can be sure the very same problems will crop up in one form or another at the Free School, too, in spite of the fact that we are so different. Here the difference is that we will help them find real solutions.

And that's the way we want it, which is why we have so few fixed rules and policies. We want there to be opportunities for things to go wrong so that kids can learn how to set them right again. This is where the idea of "therapeutic" school comes in. I place the term in quotes so that it will not suggest that we are some sort of school for problem children, which again, we most certainly are not. What we *are* is a place where it's okay to bring your problems, with "therapeutic" implying that, just as any good therapist would do, we encourage and invite the inner rumblings of the psyche to "come up." Then we work together, or struggle alone as the case may be, to take the drama all the way through to its logical conclusion, though the logic I'm speaking of here is of the inner kind where irony and paradox reign supreme.

In plain language it's called learning from your own mistakes, which many would argue is how the best learning occurs anyway. When we take on so-called problem children, we expect them to take full advantage of the available freedom and begin setting into motion a highly accelerated and imaginative course of study based entirely on personal trial and error.

I'm reminded of Terry, who must be in his mid-twenties by now. With eyes like burning coals and a ten-year-old's appealing brashness, Terry was born to rule. The only child of divorced alcoholic parents, he was sure he had already learned all there was to learn about the universe. Meanwhile, his insistence on blazing his own trail had rendered him unacceptable at his neighborhood schools and somehow he had found his way to us. Here was a boy who was as full of mischief as he was of himself, who loved to lead and whom other kids loved to follow.

You know the standard response when kids get caught in the act: "I didn't do it—he did." Or, "It was his idea." Well, as soon as Terry arrived his name began popping up in almost every one of these conversations. It was lucky for Terry that, unlike his previous places of instruction, we prefer to reward the leader and "punish" the followers. Punishment usually comes in the form of the followers having to pay the leader a small fee for his or her leadership services. Once, when we were on a weeklong expedition in the Berkshire Mountains in western Massachusetts, Terry set the all-time record for such bonuses.

Here is a perfect example of how the Free School uses paradox and metaphor to help with the healing of emotionally wounded children, whose numbers in the society seem to be growing every year. At the time we were literally blazing a trail up to the top of a secluded mountain, where we were camping out in an old converted barn on land given to Mary by her mother. Each day as we set off, it was Terry who would race to the head of the line of trail workers armed with saws, hatchets, and pruning shears. Each day the other kids would blindly follow after him, even though, being a city boy, Terry had absolutely no idea how to find his way through the forest to the site of our new trail. Finally, with a mixture of humor and exasperation—getting lost in these thick woods was no joke—we warned them that the next time they wandered off in the wrong direction behind Terry, they would each have to pay him fifty cents. Always an enterprising lad, Terry managed to collect several times during the trip and returned to school with a pocketful of cash and IOUs. The others were so mad by the end of the week that they wouldn't follow Terry anywhere for the rest of the school year.

The story continues. Not too long ago, Terry popped his head into school for a visit. Now a tall, strappingly handsome young man, he told us how he had joined the army right after graduating from high school. He said he had every intention of making a career of it, as had his grandfather, father, and several uncles before him, but after completing basic training and then trying out one of the more macho, specialized branches, he concluded that in his heart of hearts he was not a soldier after all. Somehow, he managed to extricate himself legally and honorably from the armed forces and return home. Meanwhile, the men in his family were disgusted with his choice, and Terry was struggling with their reaction.

Terry's family was close-knit, with a strong ethnic identification, and there was a lot at stake here for him. What struck me most about Terry on this day was his clarity of mind and his willingness to face head on the challenge of dealing with his disappointed elders. It was obvious that this young man was not lost at all.

A number of years ago, a couple of other men and I took a group of our more fractious Free School boys with us to a weekend "men's council" held on the ancestral land of an elderly clan mother of the Seneca Nation in western New York State. During the course of the weekend, one of our boys, who suffered from occasional volcanic rages, got into it with one of the other boys, eventually chasing after him with a pocket knife. Fortunately, two men were able to disarm Peter before anyone was hurt.

The men presiding over the council, a mix of Native Americans and non–Native Americans, were at a loss as to how best to respond to this disturbance of the peace. The mutually agreed upon prohibition against personal violence had clearly been broken. Should the boy be punished or sent home? The men from the Free School advocated for having the group of boys sit down together and talk the problem through, which they all, as it turns out, had a part in. There was general support for the idea; the only trouble was that Peter flatly refused to take part. He was still too angry, ashamed, and frightened by the power of his own reaction.

Finally, the council leader in charge of the kids decided to consult with Grandmother Twylah, who was not actively involved in the council but at whose invitation we had all come. This proved to be a very wise decision. Grandmother Twylah insisted on speaking to Peter immediately, and I ended up with the dubious honor of accompanying a very alarmed boy to her sitting room.

Easily in her seventies, Grandmother Twylah instantly melted Peter with a deeply wrinkled smile of total acceptance. She began by telling him that she sensed he had a long-standing problem controlling his temper, and he solemnly nodded his head in agreement. Then she asked him if he knew that some of the men were suggesting that he be sent home; this time he shook his head from side to side. Grandmother Twylah wouldn't allow that to happen, she explained, because she knew he had come to her land just so that this very problem could arise, giving him the opportunity to learn to deal with the force of his rage. Turning her attention to me, the clan mother explained that in the Seneca tradition, children are not punished for their wrongdoings because such acts contain a lesson. In fact, she added, life is nothing more than a series of lessons, each of which must be repeated until it is learned. Like Peter, all I could think to do was nod my head.

Native Americans appreciate the power of metaphor as well as anyone. Grandmother Twylah asked Peter if he would be willing to bury his knife under one of the old trees on her property, an act that would signal his willingness to begin learning to "bury the hatchet" whenever he found his anger being triggered. Since the pocket knife, a recent birthday gift, happened to be a prized possession, this was no easy decision. He thought for a long, silent moment before giving his consent.

Peter was not the same nine-year-old boy when he arrived back home that Sunday evening. Today he is an even-tempered eighteen-year-old, and a valued counselor at the overnight camp where he now spends his summers.

NOW, YOU MIGHT ASK, what about the other kids, the ones who don't raise hell and test the limits all the time, who want to study and attend regular classes? This is an important question and the answer is twofold. First of all, I firmly believe that it is essential for children, even younger ones, to learn to relate to and deal with all sorts of people. That's how they begin to explore the limits of their own personal power, learning who to trust and who not to trust, when to ask for help and when to go it on their own. Thus, when one of our troubled kids stirs up the pot at school, we view it as an opportunity for everyone to learn something about themselves. This brings us to one of the fundamental attributes of a true community: when one person is suffering, everyone suffers; and we can all learn from each other's mistakes.

But again, at what point does the Free School's lack of regimentation become plain unfair to the other kids? The key here, I think, is balance. If the scale tips too far toward the wild and explosive end of the spectrum, everyone can get pulled down to the level of uproar—and chaos, not learning, is the end result. We have learned over the years that sometimes it is necessary to tell a difficult child that we are just not the place for him or her. I can remember two instances in the school's history when the kids themselves actually voted chronic troublemakers out of the school. This drastic action was taken only after repeated warnings and last chances failed to bring about any change.

In the majority of these cases, troublesome kids who refuse to change decide themselves to return to the "safety" and predictability of rule-bound, heavily supervised schools. Perhaps they sense that they have come as far as they are capable of at that particular time. Ironically, those kids invariably seem to make successful transitions back to public school.

When enough of a balance is maintained, the rowdy kids on the run from schooling sooner or later find themselves drawn to the more settled kinds of learning in which so many of the others are engaged. Suddenly one day you'll see them sitting by themselves reading a book, or joining in on math classes, or launching themselves into a project of one kind or another in an area of intense interest. Or Charlene will be conducting one of her occasional poetry writing sessions and you will find them planted right next to her, pouring profound thoughts and images onto paper. Poetry, as Charlene will tell you, is often the key that opens locked doors in the mind.

In any case, it is as important not to allow resistant nonparticipants to disrupt those who want to work with focus and concentration as it is to give recent refugees from conventional schooling, or kids with a lot of anger and chaos roiling inside of them, the space to rediscover for themselves how joyful and exciting learning can be. We do the best we can with this constant interplay, and as in other areas, we take a lot of chances.

BILLY WAS A large, gawky boy who appeared dull and stupid on the surface, mildly retarded even. His face was exploding with acne and his smile was a little off center. Billy's parents had finally removed him from their local public school because of his chronic habit of inviting the abuse of the other children, who were all too happy to oblige him. One time a group of boys even threw him in a Dumpster behind the school. Meanwhile, Billy's father was schizophrenic; when he was in a bad way everyone in the family of five suffered.

Not surprisingly, given his emotional and social problems, Billy arrived at the Free School with a history of academic failure and no apparent interest in learning. Free at last, his general preference was to sit around all day and bug other kids, both as an alternative to boredom and as a sure-fire attention getter.

Thankfully—Billy's aimlessness was beginning to wear on us all—one day someone donated an old eight-track tape player with a big box of working tapes, all from the 1960s and 1970s, when Billy's father was a music-loving, dyed-in-the-wool hippy. This meant that now our lethargic lump of early teenagehood spent most of the day on his somewhat overweight derriere listening to music, a definite step in the right direction. I remained worried about him because he was years behind academically, and obviously still quite depressed. Getting him to do anything other than play his tapes was like trying to move a glacial New England boulder with a lever made of Styrofoam.

All was business as usual until he got it in his eternally earphoned head to hold a dance at the school, with himself as the DJ. Lo and behold, the dance was a great success, and suddenly Billy had a standing with his fellow students that he had never in his life enjoyed.

Hoping to build on his initial success as a disc jockey, I thought to ask Billy if he might want to apprentice at a local radio station, provided I could find one that would take him on. Billy's face lit up at the idea, and so I started phoning around. As luck would have it, I struck gold on the very first try. The student DJ who took my call volunteered to take Billy under his wing, and when Billy showed up for his initial session, he had him on the air within the hour. Our young apprentice went on to earn his FCC license and then to start his own radio station on the block in his neighborhood, all within three months of his debut.

Eventually, Billy outgrew the Free School and returned to public school. The move was entirely of his own creation, since neither his parents nor I believed he was ready to make the transition back to the abysmal world of failure and abuse from whence he had come.

In leaving us, Billy demonstrated just how resourceful he was. It was a real coup d'état on his part: One day, unbeknownst to anyone, he managed to persuade his aunt to take him to visit the middle school near her home. While he was there, he further convinced the aunt to claim that she was his legal guardian and enroll him on the spot. This was not as outlandish as it sounds; the aunt was always haranguing Billy's parents for allowing him to go to that school "where he does nothing all day." Billy just played her like a fiddle until he got what he wanted.

No one was more surprised than I was when I received a phone call from Billy's new principal the next day asking for his school records and for a little more information about this unusual new student. His mother and I agreed that there wasn't much else to do at this point but respect her son's determination to escape from freedom. Meanwhile, within two weeks of his cleverly orchestrated "transfer," I learned that Billy had already started a school radio station and that the principal had him "on the air" every morning broadcasting from his office before the daily announcements! What a turnaround! Billy, who like so many makes a point of keeping in touch, went on to have a perfectly successful high school career.

JOHN WAS ANOTHER boy who came to us with a great deal of emotional damage. Due to his mother's extreme neglect, the local child protection agency had taken him away from her. This was in an isolated area of upstate New York, where the family lived in Appalachia-like poverty. John's young mother sometimes worked as a prostitute in order to get by and frequently left her little boy alone to fend for himself.

John was adopted at the age of three; unfortunately, his new family was troubled as well. His adoptive father was a disabled combat veteran of the

Second World War and already in his sixties. He was an alcoholic, too, suffering, I suspect, from untreated Post-Traumatic Stress Disorder. He also had a slow-growing cancer, which meant that John was often preoccupied with fears about his new dad dying. John's adopted mother, a sensitive, quiet, insecure woman, was a full generation younger than her husband, and finally left him two years after the adoption because of his drunken abusiveness, taking John with her.

In John's case, his psychological trauma hadn't seriously hampered his mental development or his motivation to learn. It had, however, left him emotionally confused, unhappy, and unable to make friends. The only way that John could get at his buried grief, anger, and despair, was to play out a victim scenario, and much like Billy, invite his classmates to tease him and rough him up, all the while adamantly refusing to stick up for himself. Then he would isolate himself for long periods, feeling abused and neglected—an obvious reenactment of his earlier predicament.

One day John's "abusers" stood the problem on its head by calling a council meeting about his constant refusal to defend himself. Riding the horse in precisely the direction it was going, after all their caring pleas and exhortations had failed, they voted in a motion that John would have to sit alone—for as long as it took—until he called his own council meeting and got to work on changing his self-abasing pattern of behavior.

The kids' ploy worked, just as I'm sure they instinctively knew that it would. After two very stubborn days, John became so enraged at *having* to be isolated that he angrily demanded a new meeting where he proceeded to give his persecutors hell and vowed to stick up for himself from there forward.

Happily for all concerned, it was a promise John kept; he became a regular member of the gang of boys. Not long after his breakthrough, he decided to write his life story. I suggested he use the computer, and what followed were dozens of hours, day after day, spent by himself in front of a computer screen. It was wonderful to watch John's curse of self-isolation turn into an exercise in self-healing.

Eventually, John outgrew us, too, and decided to switch to another alternative school nearer to his home in the country, where he fared very well. I'm sure he's not entirely out of the woods yet; but clearly he was able to use his time with us to begin what probably will be a lifelong recovery process.

ALLAN CAME TO us at the late age of eleven, a budding young man with his mind, like Terry's, already made up about a great many things. His academic performance in public school had always been poor, as was his general attitude toward almost everything else, so when he began refusing to go to school at all, his parents decided to give us a try. Allan had suffered emotional abuse and neglect as a young child. Although his mother was a recovering alcoholic who had had years of sobriety and had recently married a man who would become a loving stepfather to Allan, he continued to display a number of psychosomatic symptoms such as nervous ticks and bedwetting. Thankfully, the ADHD label hadn't been invented yet, because Allan would have been a prime candidate for this diagnosis; he had tremendous nervous energy and rarely liked to sit still for long. His restlessness made progress in subjects such as math and reading unlikely.

Naturally there was concern about Allan's academic standing, although certainly not on Allan's part. His parents were relieved enough by the sudden reversal of his attitude toward school that they were willing to go along with our novel approach to their son's education, which consisted mainly of giving him the freedom to do whatever he wanted.

We discovered that Allan loved animals, hunting and fishing, and being out in the wild. On another of our five-day trips to Mary's farm in the Berkshires, Allan spent most of his time trying to catch small animals in homemade traps. His initial designs were crude and his attempts were unsuccessful. But then he showed up at school the following Monday morning with a book on animal trapping that he had gotten from his local library. We'd never seen him with a book before. He spent the next several weeks reading it and building the traps in our little school workshop. So much for his short attention span. Before long, he began working out his own designs, some of which were quite ingenious.

Ironically, back in Albany, helpless baby animals began falling at Allan's feet. He began investing the same intense energy that had previously been focused on killing animals into nurturing their offspring. Allan's first patient was a starling hatchling, not more than a few days old, which had probably been pushed out of the nest by its mother. I suggested he contact a wildlife rehabilitator at the State Conservation Department, who instructed him in the care and feeding of the baby bird.

I have seen countless wild birds perish under the hopeful care of well-meaning children, and I sure didn't expect this tiny, entirely featherless specimen to be any exception. But thanks to Allan's tireless parenting—including several middle-of-the-night feedings—not only did the bird survive, it thrived. When its feathers grew in sufficiently, Allan even helped the bird learn to fly.

He was well along in preparing the rapidly maturing starling for release back into the wild when tragedy struck. I had driven Allan out to the State Conservation Department so that he could show some other students the lab where he was now volunteering a couple of times a week. Allan had brought his bird along with him, as he generally did when he went anywhere, and we left it in the school van while we toured the lab. Though it was a cool day in early spring, I made the fatal mistake of not rolling the windows partway down. The van sat parked in the bright vernal sun and when we returned a half-hour later, the bird was already stricken by the heat. Allan tried frantically to save it, but we were too late. The little bird died in Allan's trembling hands. It takes a lot to make an adolescent boy cry, but cry he did, without shame.

When we got back to school, the bad news spread quickly. Before long, the entire community had joined Allan in his grief, and elaborate funeral preparations were begun. Allan fashioned a little casket out of cardboard while other kids created grave markers of all kinds. The entire school attended the solemn burial in the school's pet cemetery, which is under an old mulberry tree in my backyard.

Fortunately, it wasn't long before Allan was back in the saddle again. One morning soon after, while he was on his way to school, he happened upon an abandoned juvenile pigeon. It was in pretty bad shape, malnourished and unable to fly. This time, however, there was a happy ending. After a few weeks of Allan's restorative care, the now full-grown bird was well enough to be successfully released. Everyone saluted Allan for saving the pigeon's life; he proudly wore the hero's mantel for days afterward.

After two years with us, Allan decided that he, too, was ready to leave the nest. The call of that buzzing hive of early adolescence—the middle school—had become irresistible. I discouraged him from leaving the Free School just yet, only because he still hadn't done much to catch up academically, and I was worried he might be labeled a failure all over again.

But leave us he did; and sure enough, my fears were quickly confirmed. After a week or so, I received an irate phone call from Allan's new homeroom teacher: Hadn't we taught the boy anything while he was in our school? In my calmest, most reassuring tones, I told her some of Allan's history. Then I recounted his many accomplishments with us and explained that, while they weren't exactly in academic areas, she would begin to see a carryover as soon as Allan recovered from the shock of being back in the same kind of graded, competitive classroom where he had been so unsuccessful before. I urged her to see if they couldn't get Allan some extra help in the basic skills' areas, where he was lacking. The conversation ended on a hopeful, friendly note.

The gods were indeed with Allan. They found him the needed tutoring, and by the end of the marking period, he was passing all his subjects. Not only that, but when Allan's English teacher had the class write a two-page paper on the book of their choice, he stole the show. Entirely on his own initiative, Allan chose Rachel Carson's classic ecological warning, *Silent Spring*. He then proceeded to write an eight-page minithesis, which the teacher read to the entire class, calling it the best composition she'd ever received. Even though it was replete with spelling and grammatical errors, it was awarded a big, fat A+.

SALLY HAD BEEN a student in the school for years. In the lower grades she was a precocious, eager learner, full of energy and excitement. Then she hit the wall of adolescence and seemed to lose interest in just about everything. The teacher in me grew restive and concerned. I tried everything I could think of to find an inner spark that might be fanned back into flames, but all I ever got was smoke.

There were two things Sally spent her time doing that year when she wasn't hanging out with her friends. One was incessantly melting candle wax onto her hands and making molds of them; the other was weaving a multi-color rope on a small loom she had made out of an empty spool of sewing thread. She wove and then wove some more, until the rope stretched more than twice around the building. The school watched in amazement whenever she extended it to see how much longer it had grown.

Sally's parents were in the process of completing a lengthy and difficult divorce. That, combined with the onset of puberty, probably had a lot to do with her current impulse to withdraw into herself. Fortunately, I was able to relax my teaching drive and trust that she was doing exactly what she needed to be doing—or not doing what she didn't need to be doing, as the case may be. She continued weaving and molding right up until graduation day.

Sally entered Albany's centralized public high school the following September. While she was a perfectly competent student, by the end of the year she had grown weary of the endless routine and rote learning. She spent a year at a residential alternative school; the year after that, with her mother's help and an okay from the school superintendent, she worked out a modified homeschool program with Mary as her primary mentor. The two of them had a ball together, and Sally returned to being aggressive and joyful about learning. Upon completing high school, she was able to earn a scholarship to a well-known private university.

One day Sally came back to tell her old teachers what she thought, perhaps more than anything else, had contributed to her happy and successful transition into adulthood: It was that final year in the Free School, which she had spent, in her own words, "doing nothing."

WE CALL OURSELVES a therapeutic school not because we are a special school for problem children, or because we practice one form of therapy or another, but because we are a place where the profound healing of mind and sometimes even body frequently occurs (over the years we have helped wean numerous children off of potent asthma medications). And while the contribution of the teachers is far from insignificant, including their playing the role of therapist from time to time, so often it is the kids themselves whose instincts lead them in the right direction. Or, it is they who can get through to each other in ways adults cannot. I tried to select the preceding stories with these points foremost in mind.

The reason we pay so much attention to emotional and interpersonal issues is that we have found, over and over again, that when these issues are given sufficient value and attention, academic learning tends to flow like water. When children have the freedom to know themselves, like themselves, and belong to themselves, academic learning requires amazingly little time, certainly not the countless thousands of hours conventional schools spend. So many schools, however, because they are relentlessly driven by mandated standards—and not because they are staffed by bad people—place the cart squarely before the horse and then insist that everybody push, ignoring the spinning wheels and the ever deepening ruts. Rare are the children who have given up wanting to learn and grow; it's just that learning and growth are very difficult when kids are all tied up in knots.

The reality that mainstream educational models are designed to ignore is that human development is not a linear progression. Its course is often uncanny and deeply mysterious, like that of dreams. When we remember at the Free School to respect kids' own growth strategies—no matter how unlikely they might appear at the time—things always seem to come out right in the end.

This is not to say that we take a laissez-faire approach to education, as we are sometimes accused of. Here teachers often attempt to influence students in one direction or another—sometimes directly, sometimes indirectly; sometimes gently, sometimes not so gently. It all depends on the individual.

Above all else, the Free School strives to be a place where every one of its coparticipants can discover and explore the full range of their own unique forms of specialness. I guess that makes us a special school, after all.

5

Fear

The only thing we have to fear is fear itself.

—Franklin Delano Roosevelt

*F*ear is frightening. Worse still is the way in which it feeds on itself. The sad fact today is that we are living in a society increasingly run by fear—the fear of personal violence and crime, the fear of war and terrorism, the fear of a nuclear or eco-logical holocaust, the fear of scarcity, the fear of growing old and dying—the list could go on for pages. A substantial segment of our national economy, beginning with the insurance and ending with the security business, preys on these fears by offering us pro-tective and preventative policies, substances, and devices of every imaginable kind. Fear has become a growth industry.

The engine of compulsion-based education, too, is powered by fear—a fuel that has no half-life. Instead, given time combined with sufficient ignorance and denial, it silently proliferates in the hidden-away recesses of the mind, both individual and collective. Today, fear-based policy and decision making from the national level right down to every individual classroom has reached epi-demic proportions.

Since the Free School is an independent school, we are largely unaffected in any direct way by this trend. Still, I find us struggling daily with its many subtle and indirect effects. Even though we long ago opted out of the traditional reward-and-punishment teaching methodology that uses fear as a prime motivator, and even though we are up-front with our prospective new families right from the beginning that we will neither con nor coerce their children into learning, the distinctive odor of fear remains in the air nonetheless.

The entire nation is hung up these days on academic achievement, or the alleged lack thereof. We used to be falling behind the Russians; now it's the Japanese. Every day a new Chicken Little warns that something must be done about falling standardized test scores, which don't measure true intelligence anyway. Meanwhile, guided by that quintessentially American strategy—if what you're doing isn't working, try more of it—academic training is being foisted on defenseless preschoolers at ever earlier ages, and the call for lengthening the school year continues to grow louder.

And then comes the blame game. It's the teachers' fault for not teaching or expecting enough; it's the students' fault for not studying enough; it's the parents' fault for not caring enough; it's the country's fault for not maintaining high enough standards.

Here is the voice of fear speaking, whose reasoning is always circular. It's like the ancient image of the serpent swallowing its own tail—there's no beginning and no end, and therefore nowhere to break into the vicious cycle of negative reinforcement. If this were the end of it, if the trouble were just that massive numbers of adults had nothing better to worry about than how their children were doing in school, then there really wouldn't be that much of a problem. Regrettably, though, kids invariably become infected as well, and their natural, inborn desire and will to learn gets stifled in the process. Children, who live within the boundaries of their parents' emotional bodies, can literally smell the grown-ups' fear, and this is how it is passed on to them.

I chose the modality of smell here for a couple of reasons. First of all, fear does have a distinctive odor, a lesson well-known to anyone who has spent much time around honeybees or dogs. Secondly, the connection between the olfactory nerve and the brain is a large and evolutionarily old one. The extraordinary way in which certain smells can evoke powerful images and memories is evidence of this important mind/body interface— all the more powerful because it is an entirely unconscious response.

A parent's fear need not be spoken in order to be communicated. An anxious look, an apparently innocent question about what a child did (or didn't do) in school today, or even what *isn't* being talked about, can do the job of imprinting fear quite effectively. Oftentimes, parents aren't even aware they are expressing fear, doubt, or insecurity, and the more subtle the message—the farther out of audible range—the greater may be the impact on the receiver. Then, of course, there is the classic TV sitcom scene at report card time when the overwrought father is berating his failing son and asking

him if he wants to end up collecting garbage for a living. That kind of parental anger is obviously based on fear, but because it is blatant, it is easier for
kids to deal with.

It must be understood that our entire educational system and its methodology are based on fear. Why else would we fragment every "learning task"
into tiny bits so that no chewing is required, and then endlessly repeat it?
Why else would we so rigorously measure aptitude and achievement? Why
else would we as a nation continue to spend countless billions of dollars per
year to maintain a system that we collectively know is not meeting a vast
majority of children's and families' needs?

Fear is a potent emotion. It shunts the brain from higher-level thinking, an autonomic survival response I will describe in greater detail in a
moment. It prevents parents from thinking clearly about their children's
growth and development; hence many are unable to question the school's
assessment that their children are not performing up to some arbitrary standard. These frightened parents then frighten their children, who return to
classrooms controlled by frightened teachers, who in turn are sweating it out
under the supervision of frightened superintendents.

On and on it goes, right up to the top of a giant pyramid of fear, with
the students trapped inside—physiologically unable to think their way out of
the bind they're in. Instead, they are forced to resort to an unending array of
defensive maneuvers, each according to their underlying character structures. On one end of the spectrum, passive types anchor their resistance in
forgetting and playing dumb and not paying attention. On the other end,
aggressive ones actively rebel. They eventually opt out of the game altogether,
knowing full well the odds were always stacked against them.

Here is how fear works in the brain, which we now know is comprised
of three parts, each enfolded inside the other. As all organisms evolve, the
tendency is for them to hang on to outmoded structures, adding to and
improving them rather than casting them off altogether. This is exactly what
happened with the human brain. Its innermost core, aptly named the reptilian brain, is the original structure and is located at the base of the skull. This
ancient control center governs the central nervous system and manages our
vast array of survival instincts and behaviors. When we are generally at peace
with ourselves and our environment, the reptilian brain plays only a sup-
porting role, in deference to the higher two brain structures.

Surrounding the primitive reptilian brain is the higher mammalian
brain, or the limbic system. Here is the source of our awareness, emotions,
and intuition—where crude reptilian instincts are transformed into true
intelligence and applied to complex life situations. The limbic system maintains the immune system and the body's capacity to heal itself.

Finally, five times larger than its predecessors combined, the most recently evolved brain, or neocortex, integrates the input from its junior partners. It is home to our inventiveness, creative thinking, problem-solving abilities, and our spirituality. Again, when all is well, there is a general flow of energy and information from the lower brain to the higher, with the lower structures working in support of their new master, the neocortex, which integrates all three.

Now let's bring fear into the picture. Introduce a sufficient stress or threat and the brain suddenly goes into full retreat. Leslie Hart, author of *Human Brain and Human Learning* and advocate for what he terms "brain-compatible education," calls this self-protective reflex "downshifting." Imagine a speeding locomotive suddenly thrown into reverse, with all of that momentum going into miles of wheel spinning before there is any actual change of direction. In an instant, all of the developmental powers of the higher two brains place themselves in the service of their reptilian core, fueling the individual's territoriality and other primitive drives and defenses. Watching ten minutes of world or local news on any given evening will confirm the reality of this basic biological survival mechanism.

Or just observe for a day the antics of any so-called slow learner or problem child in any traditionally managed classroom in America. (I refuse to use any of the new, hyperspecific labels that, according to Gerald Coles in *The Learning Mystique,* have been invented to rationalize the epidemic of failure in our schools and to throw parents off the scent.) The antics of those frightened youngsters are fascinating, as they resourcefully apply their modern minds toward resisting the schooling game played in the classroom.

TOMMY WAS AN early victim of my teaching inexperience, back in the days when I still insisted on teaching things like reading and multiplication tables to kids who at that moment in time didn't want to learn them. He was a passive resister, who never outright refused to take his daily dose of lessons. Instead, this pudgy eight-year-old, who hadn't yet shed his baby fat, would sit outwardly compliant, apparently trying ever so hard and yet growing dumber by the minute. While I patiently held up the flash cards, six times three could, on any given day, equal anywhere from eight to a hundred and eight. Finally, one morning I woke up and noticed that the farther away Tommy got from the right answer, the broader was his dimpled, impish smile. Grateful for the tip, I smiled back and calmly put the flash cards away once and for all.

I had already tried all kinds of creative ways to ground Tommy in the concept of multiplication, using materials such as Cuisenaire rods and money, and all kinds of songs and games. He was simply either unready or uninterested in learning it, at least from me. Meanwhile, I never was able to determine which he was resisting, the math or me—or both. At the end of the school year his alarmed and critical father, who had divorced Tommy's mother a couple of years earlier, intervened and insisted he be placed in public school. Tommy's dad came from good conservative, working-class Irish Catholic stock, and was vocally concerned about his firstborn son's lack of academic progress.

Looking back, Tommy was probably mildly dyslexic, a term I am occasionally willing to use in referring to children since at least it accurately describes a specific state of affairs. Though you won't find it in the 1963 edition of *Webster's Collegiate Dictionary*, which sits on the shelf above my writing desk, the word only means "difficulty with reading." Tommy's response to mandatory reading lessons was more or less identical to the math ones.

I was sorry to see Tommy go for several reasons. First of all, he was in many ways a gifted child. He had unusual artistic talent and was already showing signs of athletic potential. He was also winsome and likable and was missed by all long after he was gone. And as in several cases already cited, I was afraid he wouldn't respond well to a learning environment based on full-time compulsion, where the opportunity for him to pursue his strengths would be circumscribed at best.

At the time I felt I had failed miserably with Tommy. This was before I had enough experience with children to know that they learn when they want to and when they're ready. Tommy wasn't dumb at all; his lack of progress had just been his way of saying, "No, Chris, I'm sorry, but I don't want to memorize my times tables right now. I want to paint and draw and run and wrestle. Maybe later, okay?" He expressed his resistance by shutting off the power to that part of his neocortex responsible for the storage and retrieval of bits of data. Moreover, I wasn't a bad teacher. My methods were fine. I liked Tommy. I didn't get angry with him and put him down. And I didn't frighten his parents with the notion that their son was suffering from some sort of mental disability.

In the end, Tommy's transfer to public school was probably for the best. His dad was both pleased and relieved by the move, which meant that Tommy no longer had to carry the heavy burden of his father's anxiety and displeasure. The ethic of the public school was more consonant with the father's fear-driven belief system, where school is work and work is something that you have to do, so you just damn well better do it. Tommy would eventually learn his multiplication tables, but schoolwork remained a struggle for him right on through high school. Fortunately, his artistic gifts continued to unfold despite his academic difficulties, and he became a championship-caliber wrestler. Unfortunately, his father—like so many parents who are worried about their offspring's future success—used Tommy's participation in sports as the carrot at the end of the stick; his successful school careers in football and wrestling both came to a premature end when he continued to fail one or another of his subjects each term.

JUST WHAT ROLE does fear play in a little school like ours, where learning is regarded as a natural, joyful process? The answer brings to the surface another important paradox. While our informal, organically structured, family-like environment readily defuses the stored-up fear of a recent refugee from public school, it often has the opposite effect on the parent(s). The litany of questions, spoken or unspoken, revealing their fear goes something like this: Where are the textbooks? What about homework? What if my child just decides to play all day? How will I know he is learning if there are no grades or report cards? What will happen when she goes back to a regular school?

These are all legitimate questions, appropriate expressions of concern about a child's well-being. I strive to answer them honestly and compassionately, sometimes addressing the subject of fear head-on, and other times responding in a more roundabout way, depending on the degree of fear I sense. Twenty-four years of dancing with the dragon have taught me that corrosive fear transcends all lines of race and class. The biggest common denominator is parents' own schooling histories. Whenever fearful parents talk about their childhood experiences in school, I discover they encountered the same struggles as their kids, and furthermore that they, too, had parents who worried about their educational development. Such fertile soil for the seeds of fear to sprout in the next generation.

To reassure anxious parents, I try to find an effective way to get across to them something I learned from Joseph Chilton Pearce at a workshop for teachers here in Albany a number of years ago. Pearce says that all children are "hardwired" to learn, by which he means that children's in-born programming automatically gears them for learning, a process we now know begins in utero to a truly astonishing degree. Understanding this, it becomes more a question of how we manage to keep kids *from* learning, rather than how they learn in the first place. Pearce's belief, based on extensive new research into the psychobiology of the mind, is that each child already contains his or her God-given potential, and that what we call "learning" is the natural unfolding of that potential. This, of course, brings us back to the true meaning of the word *education*, which derives from the Latin *educare*, meaning "to lead out."

Pearce added one important qualifier to his notion of hardwired learning: intelligence will fully unfold if and only if the environment resonates with children according to their individual nature and developmental timetable. It's not hard to see how monumental an "if" this is. For instance, at birth the learning that has already begun in the womb as the fetus responds to cues from the mother's body—heartbeat, voice, emotional states—as well as those of the father and siblings, is often crashingly interrupted by modern, "scientific," birth practices. A newborn infant's early developmental surge depends entirely on complete and immediate bonding with the mother, to which the hospital routine is inherently antagonistic. The medical model, too, is rooted in fear; its practitioners waste little time transmitting that fear to the recipients of their care.

And this is just the beginning of a series of impediments to the real and sustained nurturing that little children need in order to develop into complete selves. Next, day care, television, and all of the enticements and artificial substitutes of a consumer culture take our children into their bloodless arms, leaving us with an entire generation of children with one strike against them. This gives parents like Tommy's dad ample reason to be concerned about their children's future and sets the wheel of fear into motion.

YEARS LATER, ANOTHER budding young artist would come to me at the beginning of the school year and ask me to organize a math class, so that she could prepare herself for the transition to public high school the following September. With us since the age of four, Abby was a tall, bouncing, happy sort who possessed a wonderfully quirky sense of humor. Like Tommy, she generally got on well with everyone. And like so many artists, she had an intense inner life, which she loved to make visible in her art.

When Abby had first become a "downstairs kid," meaning when she moved from the preschool into the elementary section of the school, she showed little interest in reading, writing, or math, preferring instead to spend countless hours immersed in imaginative play with the other children, or alone with her doodling pad and her daydreams. Rosalie was her primary teacher that year and this was fine with Abby. Occasionally, Rosalie would try to entice Abby into scholarly pursuits, but the child's response was lukewarm at best. Six continues to be a magical age and Rosalie was quite content to sit back and play mother hen to her little group, all of whom were magical children indeed.

I remember doing a little math with Abby from time to time. At seven, she knew her numbers, could count to a hundred, and was able to learn to add and subtract without too much difficulty. However, she was showing certain signs of stress and disinterest, which would become more and more the case as the concepts became more complex. Eventually she drifted away from the subject altogether.

Reading was pretty much the same story. Although Abby was from a reading family and loved being read to, she didn't make much progress toward "breaking the code" for several years. She even exhibited some of the textbook symptoms of dyslexia such as letter, number, and word reversals, and the inability to transfer what she had managed to retain from one level to the next.

Naturally, this aroused concern in her parents, and to a certain extent, in her teachers. But thanks to good communication and rapport between home and school—plus a basic faith in Abby's intelligence and her will to learn and grow—we were able to keep our collective fear in check. Unfortunately, the picture was not so simple. Abby's grandmother was a retired remedial reading specialist, and she became quite alarmed when Abby reached the age of eight and was still not reading competently. Quickly, the grandmother's fear began to spread to Abby's parents. It was here that I began my course in Fear 101.

Mary, who was now retired from daily teaching but with whom we consulted frequently, was convinced that a team of wild horses wasn't going to keep Abby from learning to read. She continued to urge everyone to keep their cool and let nature take its course. Meanwhile, however, the grandmother's fears were beginning to take their toll. Abby's parents finally decided to hire a reading tutor for her, and Abby's mom began teaching her at home, using the remedial exercises sent to her by her increasingly anxious mother. When there was little demonstrable progress on Abby's part, the situation became ripe for diagnosing Abby with a bona fide "reading problem." It was at this point that Abby's grandmother offered to travel to Albany to give us a workshop in remedial reading, and Mary wisely counseled us to accept her offer. Our openness to her input lessened her anxiety considerably and cut significantly into the transmission of fear from grandmother to mother to child.

In the end, Abby didn't learn to read until she was nine or ten. *How* she learned may remain a mystery. Had the tutoring finally taken hold? Was it the grandmother's expertise? Was it the poetry sessions in which Charlene wrote out Abby's award-winning poetry and in which together they created books and magazines out of Abby's exquisite words and drawings? Or was it simply a matter of allowing Abby to learn to read in her own time and in her own way? Perhaps it was all of the above.

As so often happens with so-called late readers, it happened quickly. When Abby did begin reading on her own, she and good books were suddenly inseparable. All at once, it seemed, she was voraciously reading long novels written for children her age or older. It is critical to note here that nothing was ever done without Abby's full consent and willing participation (she liked her reading tutor and thoroughly enjoyed their time together), so that learning to read never became an onerous chore. Also, she was never confronted with the judgment that she was in some way defective. I know many people who were force-fed reading in school who now find little pleasure in what should be a lifelong source of inspiration and delight.

Getting back to that math class Abby had asked me to teach, I found her waiting for me at the table at the very beginning of the first session. She had arrived before any of the others, and her tears were already pooling up on the old, tattered workbook she had brought with her, a relic of that earlier time before she had decided to put math aside. I sat down next to her and quietly asked what was the matter. She answered that she was afraid she couldn't learn math, that it was just too hard for her. We talked about her earlier difficulties with reading and I reminded her how quickly she had learned to read once she was ready. I told her it was perfectly okay that she was setting out at this point to tackle math—I had seen others her age do the same—and that she had probably been wise to wait until the math-learning circuits in her brain were more complete. Together we agreed that fear was her real problem.

This time around was an entirely different story. Abby quickly discovered that she *could* do math and that it was actually fun. When she managed to memorize the multiplication tables in less than a week, it was all downhill from there. There was no sign of her earlier memory "dysfunction"; and while she still didn't quite pick up new concepts as quickly as the kids for whom math was a breeze, her attitude remained positive and her progress steady. Abby's goal was to be up to grade level by the end of the school year. Come June she was solving algebraic equations with relative ease.

Abby was noticeably anxious as well as excited about moving on to the brave new world of public school. Her big worry remained whether she would be able to keep up academically, but her fears proved to be unfounded. Abby's name could be seen on the honor roll at the conclusion of her very first term and stayed there for good. She continued to excel creatively, at one point winning a scholarship to a prestigious summer camp for gifted young artists.

FEAR AND LEARNING make lousy dance partners. Count Abby among the lucky ones whose parents and teachers were able to keep their fear in check and allow her to develop according to her own internal schedule. Perhaps even more important, they managed to maintain their belief that Abby's learning belonged to her. When she learned, it was for her own reasons. At every turn, the motivation came from within and not from without.

This point cannot be stressed enough. In *Punished by Rewards: The Trouble with Gold Stars, Incentive Plans, "A's," Praise and Other Bribes,* Alfie Kohn cites study after study documenting how individuals—children in school or adults in the workplace—whose performance is based on extrinsic rewards and punishments do far less well than those who are self-motivated and who find their satisfaction in the activity itself. Kohn points out how the inhibitory effects of negative reinforcement were demonstrated decades ago by B. F. Skinner, the inventor of behaviorism—the chosen psychology of conventional schooling. He then proceeds to reveal his own research, which shows that even such simple forms of positive reinforcement as praise can significantly hamper learning and achievement.

The reason for this, I am convinced, is fear, which we now know is biologically incompatible with learning. The managed, monitored, and measured learning environments of most modern schools communicate an unspoken fear that says that without all the trappings of regimentation, nothing constructive would ever happen. Such a model remains deeply rooted in the Hobbesian notion that children, left to their own devices, can't be trusted to learn a damn thing in preparation for the nasty, brutish, and short life predicated by the prominent seventeenth-century rationalist philosopher.

The antidote to fear is trust. Unfortunately, unlike so many other remedies these days, it doesn't come in a capsule. Nor have I seen any self-help manuals on ten easy steps to trust. There are no money-back guarantees either. Trust involves a certain amount of the unknown and the unknown implies risk. Nevertheless, when we take that leap of faith and trust children to assume responsibility for themselves, they learn more quickly and more easily, and the learning tends to be for life and not just until the end of the marking period. Abby and countless other Free Schoolers from over the years stand today as living proof.

6

Concentration

ake three adults and twenty-five urban, inner-city, and suburban kids of all sizes, shapes, and colors to 250 acres on a
reforested mountaintop. Drill 9/16" diameter holes in the
south sides of some healthy sugar maple trees. Tap in the spiles
and hang lidded buckets from the hooks. Thank the trees. Gasp
when you see the first droplets of sap spurt forth. Pray for the
right cycling of freeze and thaw, freeze and thaw to keep the sap
dripdripdripping into the pails. Empty them when they're full.
Haul the heavy sap in plastic five-gallon buckets to the storage
barrels near the evaporator and pour in the precious tree-blood.

Repeat all but steps one, two, and three as necessary. Oh, and
remember to take a long guzzle of the ice-cold, sweet crystalline
liquid every time you empty the pails (to keep the doctor away).

When the fifty-five-gallon drums are nearly full, scour the
forest for fallen branches or standing dead trees. Drag them over
to the arch. Saw them into lengths with two-person bow saws (a
chain saw will ruin everything). Learn how to work together and
discover the difference between good wood and rotten wood,
which yields no heat when burned. Drag more branches. Trip
over the underbrush and get your face scratched. Or get your boot
sucked off by the deep, wet snow. Delete a few expletives. Saw
more wood. . . . "I NEED MORE WOOD NOW! DO YOU WANT
THE FIRE TO GO OUT? HURRY UP!!" ("But I'm cold, but I'm
tired, but she/he's not doing anything, but I can't find my mittens,
but . . . but . . .")

Take a break and start a snowball war. Play in the huge mud puddle next to the road. Salute the sun when it finally breaks free from the cold gray clouds (no New Age—or Old Age—adult-inspired pseudorituals allowed, either; just young children off by themselves spontaneously breaking into song when they suddenly find themselves wrapped in the sun's warm embrace). Eat large quantities of good food. Drink some more sweet sap.

Try to get a very big, very hot fire going with a lot of damp, soggy fuel. Discover that the dead lower branches of pine trees make fire medicine, and that birch bark is even better if you can find it. Learn how to strike a kitchen match without burning yourself. Once the fire's going, pour ten gallons of the maple sap into a two-foot-by-three-foot pan (the evaporator), which rests a bit precariously over the fire on two rows of cinderblocks (the arch). Endlessly debate whether a watched pot ever boils. Come back and sit by the fire and feed it twigs whenever you get cold (the fire remains at the center of the dance throughout). Watch for patterns in the billowing steam and get smoke in your eyes. Poke a stick into the murky, bubbling mess and taste the gathering sweetness. Ask if it's syrup yet a few dozen times throughout the day and night. Find out that it really does take forty gallons of sap to make just one gallon of syrup.

Watch the sun set and the first star appear. Don't forget to make a wish. Let the darkness gradually creep up and enfold you. When it starts to turn cold again, try to remember where you left your coat and hat. If your feet are wet, go put on dry socks; if your boots are wet on the inside, put plastic bags on your feet before you put your boots back on. Come back out and discover that dry cattail heads make excellent torches if you have enough imagination. Watch the swarm of excited fireflies darting around the fire in the winter/spring moonlight. Oh, and don't forget the moon—get out a good telescope and study her up real close for the first time. And search for Jupiter and Saturn, too. Wonder about the stars and the planets and the whole universe. Ask all the questions, even the why ones that have no answers. Wonder some more.

Get very tired—the good kind of tired. ("It's still not syrup yet?") Go back inside the old lodge and make up a warm bed as near to the wood-stove as you can. If you're missing your mommy or your daddy, notice how that feels in your body, and where. (Is there anyone in the room who can give you the right kind of comfort when you're this vulnerable?) Let someone read you a Grimm's fairy tale before you fall into a deep, dreamful sleep.

Wake up in the morning and finish off enough syrup on the kitchen stove for a victory pancake breakfast. Celebrate! WE DID IT!! That thickened, amber concentrate is its own sweet reward for a long hard day's work and play, with its measure of physical and psychic discomfort. Have another pancake or just keep sticking your finger in the syrup pot and licking it until your teeth begin to ring. Celebrate!

MAPLE SUGARING IS both an exciting activity for kids and a wonderful metaphor for the educational process. First of all, I want to play with this notion of concentration. I'm not referring to an intense mental act or the old television game show where you had to remember the location of the other half of the match in order to win the prize. Here I'm thinking about how you get to the essence of something. Or, put another way, how you get the most out of what you have to work with.

It's no secret that there is an ever increasing gap in our modern world between experience and meaning. And because children today face ever increasing levels of distraction—to the point of encountering "virtual reality"—I am afraid that their ability to distinguish between what is important and what is unimportant will be ever diminishing. Seen in this light, it seems to me that any true definition of education must include a description of the process whereby one gradually discovers how to skim off the dross in order to get to the precious metal underneath, or how to boil down one's experience until what's left is essential.

This is why we bring kids out to Rainbow Camp, our semiwilderness "school-away-from-school" in the New York foothills of the Berkshire Mountains. The rambling old lakeside lodge, in constant need of repair, has gradually replaced Mary's family farm in Massachusetts as the setting for our version of what is commonly known today as "outdoor education."

The time we spend at the camp is an integral part of what we do. It is a place where I have witnessed personal revolutions in dozens of children over the years. The reason for this, I am quite certain, is the fact that everyone suddenly finds themselves displaced from their familiar patterns, with very few props to fall back on. For example, there's no television or radio, and we heat with wood. Also, there's no running water in the wintertime. Water for flushing toilets has to be hauled from one of the nearby brooks that feed the lake, meaning that the repercussions of wasting water are very physical indeed. Everyone quickly learns the first law of water conservation: *if it's yellow let it mellow, if it's brown flush it down.*

It's much like nineteenth-century rural farm life. We live as a sprawling extended family, with even the youngest sharing the cooking, cleaning, and

wood-and water-gathering chores, and the oldest often reading bedtime stories to the younger kids. It can be a lot of hard work, especially during sugaring season, when everyone's stamina is put to the test.

THERE'S NO FORMULA for what we do at Rainbow Camp, because there
life is governed by the needs of the moment. Two terms used by Wilhelm
Reich in the 1930s at least partially describe what we're up to, *self-regulation*
and *work democracy*. The idea behind self-regulation is that if kids can
learn—and the earlier the better—how to manage their own rhythms, how
to make responsible choices by learning from the consequences of their own
or someone else's mistakes, and how to meet their own needs, they will be
better equipped to become autonomous adults capable of authoring satisfying and meaningful lives. At a lecture A. S. Neill gave in London on the subject of Summerhill, Reich was thrilled to learn about a school that operated
according to this principle.

Reich coined the term *work democracy* after attempting to effect mass
social change in Europe through the political systems of several countries. He
eventually became disillusioned, concluding that power politics under any
banner, no matter how "socially democratic," always end up standing in the
way of real solutions to social problems. Work democracy, on the other
hand, is the notion that when groups of people organize themselves around
common tasks and goals, natural forms of authority and decision making
that support mutual accomplishment will emerge. In a true work democracy,
cooperation rather than competition is a core value.

Life at Rainbow Camp is not always "democratic," at least not in the
way the term is most commonly used today. Often the demands of daily
living require that kids and grown-ups alike do things they would just as
soon not do right then and there. Sometimes we just put kids to work. No
meetings, no votes—we simply say, "Please do it!" and expect that it will
get done.

This sometimes comes as a rude surprise to first-timers at the camp
who are used to being indulged at home, a pattern that appears to be on the
rise regardless of social class. I once had three young rebels, all recently
arrived from public school, who refused to carry any firewood in for the
night. When I told them there would be no lunch for them until they did, all
three vowed to walk the twenty-five miles home to Albany. After they were
about a mile down the road, I picked them up in the van and told them I
would have to have an okay from their mothers before I could let them continue on their way. Left to choose between firewood or phoning home, they
decided on the former. Then they had the time of their lives for the remain-

der of our stay, busily climbing tall pine trees and endlessly roaming the woods in search of adventure.

Another time, Rakeem, a baby-faced eleven-year-old inner-city parochial school cast-off, helplessly decided that he couldn't stuff his borrowed sleeping bag into its generously large sack. Rakeem's strategy was to foist the unstuffed bag back on the much smaller boy from whom he had borrowed it. That youngster could have, and I'm sure would have, called a council meeting; but since everyone was so busy packing for home, I very undemocratically decided to intervene.

I had an instinct that this was just the moment for me to put Rakeem, who had a smothering mother and no father, into a bind instead. I told him that the borrowed bag was certainly his to deal with and that he would get no breakfast until he had all of his gear in order. Predictably, Rakeem, who was overweight and chronically angry, stomped off upstairs to curse and sulk. Breakfast time drew near, and with still no sign of our boy, I announced I was ready to bet cash that Rakeem was about to miss a meal. Immediately, Isaac, who had come to us from the same parochial school, held out his hand and yelled, "Dollar bet!" We shook on it and then went about our business.

When another five minutes went by and there was still no sign of Rakeem, I told Isaac that he'd better get his money together, because breakfast was ready. He quickly bolted up the stairs. Rakeem appeared within moments, breathless. He stuffed the bag and returned it to its owner. There was delight and laughter all around when I presented Isaac with a crisp new dollar bill.

Ironically, it was Isaac who had called a council meeting about Rakeem just the night before, because Rakeem had bullied him out of one of the camp's cozy armchairs by the woodstove. At that meeting, Isaac managed to pass a motion that Rakeem, who sullenly stonewalled when asked by the other kids what was up, would have to sit in the very chair he had taken from Isaac—all night, if necessary—until he called another meeting to work out the problem (which he eventually did). As I paid off my bet, I made sure to point out to Rakeem what a true friend he had in Isaac—on two counts now.

I thing Reich would view our antics at Rainbow Camp as self-regulation and work democracy in action. There it is essential that we all act responsibly and all pull together. Most kids catch on quickly. Meanwhile, at both the camp and at school we try not to adhere too rigidly to any ideological precepts: "democracy," "work democracy," or otherwise. Even the best of ideas tends to turn toxic when practiced in a worshipful, fundamentalistic way.

This brings me to a bone I have to pick with old Neill on the subject of children and work. He wrote in *Summerhill* that if you ever see a child working voluntarily, you are looking at a kid who has in some way been brainwashed by an adult. According to Neill, for healthy, free children, work is a four-letter word. I don't entirely disagree with him, but my years at the Free School have taught me something different. Neill was a rebel at heart, and Summerhill has always been populated largely by rebellious middle- and upper-middle-class children. I think these factors may have colored his conclusions on this score.

I have observed kids working, by choice and with great gusto and plea-sure, on a great many occasions. But several factors must be in place to make this so: First of all, the work has to be organic; that is, it has to have inherent meaning to the kids *on their terms*. Also, they have to be free to continually change the way and the pace at which they go about the job, whatever it might be. Certainly, free children hate just about anything when it becomes routine. Sometimes I just have to bite my tongue whenever I'm tempted to suggest a better, faster, more efficient way to get the job done, because when I do intrude, invariably their enthusiasm disperses as fast as the air out of an untied balloon. Finally, the fruits of their labors need to follow directly from the completion of the task.

Maple sugaring serves as a perfect example. The kids are enthralled by the magic of the process—the fire, the transmutation of the sap, the late nights—and then each of them gets to take home a small jar of syrup to share with their families. Later, they help with marketing the rest to raise cash toward fixing up the camp. Kids love making money, even when it goes to the school rather than into their own coffers.

My experience tells me there is an important relationship between work and meaning. The problem is that our increasingly materialistic and secular culture tends to ignore the connection between the two. Real work, that which has tangible purpose and is accompanied by a sense of accom-plishment, is disappearing as fast as our natural resources. One solution is to provide children with the opportunity to work and to experience the corre-sponding satisfaction of a job well done.

ACTUALLY, VERY LITTLE time is taken up by chores at Rainbow Camp. Most of it we spend fishing, swimming, boating, walking or racing through the woods, learning about wildflowers and edible plants, exploring the old cemetery adjacent to the property, gazing at the moon, stars, and planets at night—with or without the six-foot telescope someone gave us—and listen-ing to stories at bedtime.

Much like at school, each day structures itself; the right things seem to happen when they need to. For instance, it was Alexandra, a nine-year-old girl who had accidentally set fire to her bedroom three years before, who kept turning up to help tend the fire in the arch. She had been absolutely ter-rified of fire ever since the incident. At one point, when the two of us were alone, I was able to find just the right opening for talking through her fire-setting experience with her. It seemed important for her to return to that traumatic event and explore its teachings. Our talk was easy and relaxed, and all the while Alexandra steadily pushed back the edge of her fear by tending and feeding the fire that was concentrating our syrup and warming us against the night.

Then there was Anton, a six-year-old boy who the year before had been taken away from and then returned to his mother—thanks, in part, to our intervention on the family's behalf—by the Department of Social Services. He was the last one to go in one night while I was pushing to finish boiling off a batch of sap. Anton sat quietly for hours, poking the fire with one stick after another while I talked about everything under the moon with Mark, a recent college graduate who was volunteering at the school. There was nowhere else Anton wanted to be at that moment. What was he, fatherless like Rakeem, learning while he sat there listening to two men talking and laughing in low tones? One can only imagine, but my guess is that, among other things, he was studying how two men go about getting to know each other better.

ONE OF MY favorite stories to tell kids when we stay overnight at Rainbow Camp making maple syrup is Grimm's "The Water of Life". It contains many interior meanings, and it also beautifully brings home my theme here. The story goes like this:

> Once there were three princes, whose father was slowly wasting away from some mysterious ailment. While the three young men grieved away, an old man came along one day and told them that there existed a cure for the king. Known as the Water of Life, it could only be attained after a long journey. The oldest son, anxious to gain the favor of his father, was the first to go in search of the cure. Soon after setting out, he came across a dwarf waiting beside the road. When the dwarf asked where he was headed, the prince only sneered at him; the insulted and enraged dwarf placed a very effective curse of imprisonment on him. The very same thing happened to the second son. When he also failed to return home, the youngest son set off. He, too, encountered the dwarf. But unlike his older brothers, he stopped and told the dwarf the whole story. Then he asked for his help. The dwarf told the young prince that the Water of Life could only be found in a certain enchanted castle, and he gave the prince exactly the tools he would

need to survive the trials that lay ahead. The prince survived and found the castle. There he met a beautiful princess, who promised him her kingdom if he would free her from the spell by coming back in a year's time to marry her. She told him where to find the well containing the special water. He filled a cup with it and headed home. Passing the dwarf along the way, the prince stopped to thank him and to ask if he happened to know where were his two brothers. The dwarf told him about the curse and the prince begged for their release, which the dwarf granted—but not before warning the young man about his older brothers' bad hearts. Soon enough, both brothers did betray their naive younger sibling, tricking him out of the healing water and using it to win favor from their father. Then each, in turn, went off to win the princess for himself. Unbeknownst to them, however, the princess, who was most anxious for the return of her prince, had ordered the road leading to the palace to be paved with gold. She instructed the guards to admit only the man who rode straight up the middle of the road to her gate, as only he would be her true lover. When the oldest brother saw the golden road, he stopped to admire it and decided it would be a shame to ride upon it. He rode to the right of it instead, and was turned away by the castle guards. Next came the second brother, who was equally desirous of the gold in the road. He decided to ride to the left of it and was also turned away. Meanwhile, the young prince, having now survived an entire year in bitter exile, decided to seek out the princess before it was too late. So intent was he on joining with her beauty that he never even saw the golden road. He galloped straight down the middle to the gate, where he was immediately admitted by the guards. After he and the princess were married, the young prince decided to rejoin his now-healed father, who had since learned of the older sons' deceit and was eager to welcome home his true savior.

I like this story so much because, in it, the young prince, as a result of great hardship and travail, becomes *concentrated*. He is so focused on what is essential in his life that nothing can keep him from his goal. Moreover, the "heat" generated by his troubles and his great yearnings are necessary elements in his growth.

This is what makes making maple syrup such a perfect metaphor for the educational process. Getting to the essence of something, and more important, to the essence of who we are, requires effort, hard work, perseverance, and sometimes suffering. That's why we try to spend a week or two every spring turning the water of life of the sugar maple tree into thick, sweet, amber-gold syrup.

7

Metaphors Within Metaphors

All of a sudden I turned into a rainbow
I am all different colors
When I come out, people look at me
They say I look pretty
I am magical
I come out every morning
And people see me get happy

—Ghirmay Ghidei

*T*his poem has been growing yellowed and wrinkled while thumbtacked to our bedroom wall for nearly twenty years. It was written by a former student, a troubled boy of six who lived with my wife and me for a time. Ghirmay had pretty much been abandoned by his Ethiopian father and was one of three children of a young welfare mother of southern Italian descent who was struggling with alcohol addiction. Ghirmay had not been having an easy time of it, to say the least. At one point, he even lost most of his hair due to stress-related alopecia. It has since grown back and he is now quite a handsome young man.

I chose the poem because, in addition to being very dear to my heart, it is a good example of how central metaphor is in children's lives. For this reason, we see it as one of our primary purposes at the Free School to provide each child with the space—both physical and existential—to invent, tear down, and experiment with many metaphors of their own making.

This is why you will find our kids, particularly the younger ones, spending so much time lost in imaginative play. Nowhere is the experimentation with metaphor more obvious than when children are playacting and dressing up. To facilitate this essential kind of learning, we always keep two large trunks on each floor of the building, filled with costumes and accessories of every imaginable kind, including a set of exotic, lacy gowns donated to us by a bridal shop that went out of business. Of course there is a large mirror on the wall for carefully studying "the look." Inevitably, the costuming inspires the spinning of a tale or fantasy of one kind or another, and occasionally a finished product emerges, which might then be staged before the school's best audience—the preschoolers—who love nothing more than a spontaneous live production and who are most uncritical.

This is also why we never turn writing and the other expressive arts into academic exercises. When children aren't forced to write, and when spelling and grammar take a backseat to meaning, mood, and image, young writers work almost reflexively in metaphor, thanks to their natural identification with animals, colors, sounds, and so on. Perhaps this approach to writing gives our kids an unfair advantage when they enter city-wide poetry contests, and explains how come they frequently walk away with more than their fair share of prizes.

EARLIER I TOLD the story of Tommy, a resistant learner whose father removed him from our school. This was back in the days when we were less confident in our unorthodox approach to education, when some of the kids' learning activities were compulsory, and they generally spent the entire morning under the charge of one teacher. Tommy was actually one of eight seven-, eight- and nine-year-olds in my group, several of whom were just coming off unhappy public school experiences.

Far more troubling to me than Tommy's and some of the others' reluctance to learn basic academic skills was the fact that these kids seemed incapable of getting along with each other. They argued, bitched, and bickered incessantly. And that was on good days. Finally, in near desperation, I decided to give up everything else I was trying to do with them and began to read aloud to any of them who wanted to listen. I selected a juicy, exciting classic: George McDonald's *The Princess and Curdie,* a children's romance full of intrigue and magical beings, with a girl and a boy protagonist the same age as the kids in the group.

When about half of them began wandering in and out of the room over the course of the first few chapters, I grew a bit doubtful of my choice of novels. It was written in turn-of-the-century English, a style quite foreign to the kids. My fears were somewhat laid to rest when I realized that the student most tuned in to the story was Franz, the boy who had been giving me—and everyone else—the hardest time. Still struggling with reading at the age of eight, Franz was hanging on to every word. His ability to understand the difficult syntax and to follow McDonald's long descriptive passages was extraordinary, and his enthusiasm became contagious. Before long, all of the children were glued to their seats again, insisting I read for the entire morning.

As the story drew to a dramatic and happy ending, I found myself deluged with a chorus of pleas to help them act the narrative out. Still a bit shell-shocked by this defiant bunch, I decided to play hard to get. I told them that the story was too complex, and besides, it was a novel and not a play. They disagreed emphatically, and said that they would create the dialogue and ask Missy, our art teacher, to help them make props, scenery, and costumes. Before I realized what was happening, they had organized themselves into a cast. I was appointed director and instructed to write everything down.

Suddenly it was *my* turn to get into the flow. Before my very eyes these cantankerous kids, who previously couldn't even cross the street together without battling for position, had sorted out their roles for the play—some of them taking on three or four parts—with hardly a single argument.

When things quieted down and I had a chance to reflect on what was taking place, I began to notice that the children all had chosen precisely the right roles for themselves. Franz, who was not well liked because of his constant teasing and bullying, was the unanimous choice to play the leading role of Curdie, who undergoes an important change of heart during the course of the story. When work on the play began, Franz was still struggling with remembering how to spell his last name, and here the class was clamoring for an all-out adaptation of a very long and complicated story, with Franz responsible for a majority of the lines, including numerous long speeches taken verbatim from the novel. To top it all off, the kids decided they wanted to invite parents, grandparents, friends, and neighbors to a gala evening performance of the production, thereby increasing the pressure on themselves (and me) a hundredfold.

Clearly, there was a small miracle under way. Franz, to whom the idea of reading or any kind of schoolwork had previously been anathema, began going home and studying his lines every night. At one point he was having terrible trouble memorizing one particularly long and difficult speech, so I suggested that we rewrite it in his own words to make it easier to remember. He came in the next day able to recite the original version word for word!

Then there was Alicia, another struggling new student who was always on the fringe, preferring either to be alone or to play with much younger children whom she could easily dominate. She was also a reluctant reader, who generally came to school looking like an unmade bed. Naturally, she elected to play the female lead, which is the complex dual role of an ancient and mystical grandmother/queen and the beautiful young granddaughter/ princess who saves the day, aided by the magical powers of her grandmother. Alicia demonstrated amazing inner flexibility and control as she alternated between the two parts; she, too, was absolutely determined to overcome her so-called reading handicap and learn every one of her numerous lines. Also, she began coming to school each day, much to the delight of her exasperated mother, with her hair beautifully brushed and parted.

Mark, always mousy and shy, elected to play the role of the evil Lord Chamberlain, who betrays Curdie. Before long he was astounding everyone in rehearsals as he started to ham it up, shouting out his lines to an imaginary back row. Bryn, a diminutive, blond-haired, blue-eyed "good little girl," typecast by the others as the young princess in the play, began to rebel and to assert herself. She refused to sit back and watch the climactic final battle as McDonald had written it, and instead insisted on slashing away with her dagger right alongside the boy/warriors. She also didn't want to marry Curdie in the end, and so we changed that part, too.

Philip, a talented but very angry boy, chose to play both the roles of the wise king and the traitorous butler who takes part in the plot to poison him. In the end, the king manages to harness his rage at being betrayed by those close to him. Thanks to his self-control, he is able to drive the evil forces from the kingdom. James, on the other hand, who ordinarily kept his anger and aggression tightly under wraps, got so into the role of the devious royal physician that, during the performance, the audience hissed loudly every time he appeared onstage, especially when he attempted to stab the king.

Michael was a one-of-a-kind, oddball sort of kid. I don't think he liked himself very much, and so he tended to act strangely in order to win attention. In the play, he cleverly improvised one of the strange, magical monster-creatures who help Curdie defeat the enemy. Creating that role, which he pulled off with great aplomb, seemed to me to be his way of getting at his wounded self-image. Then there was Tyrone, with a hot-tempered father and an idolized older brother in whose shadow he angrily lived, choosing to play the role of Peter, Curdie's kind and reasonable father. During the performance, when he heroically arrives in the nick of time to rescue Curdie, his entrance was so total that it practically carried him into the laps of the onlookers in the front row, where his big brother sat proudly watching.

Finally, there was big Tommy, playing Lina, Curdie's lovable, wolflike guardian, who becomes a central hero-figure as the story develops. Although it was a nonspeaking role (he continued to shy away from nonphysical challenges), Tommy received one of the loudest ovations as the curtain fell.

It was a magnificent performance, played to a standing-room-only crowd in a makeshift theater on the second floor of the school. Ovation after ovation provided the kids with a well-deserved acknowledgment for their months of dedicated work. It had not been easy, and they had challenged themselves in every imaginable respect. Though there was no shortage of ruffled feathers along the way, especially as the tension of performing before a live audience mounted, they had absolutely amazed me with their ability to work together.

But what impressed me most of all was the way in which the kids had used the interplay with personal metaphor to experiment with new ways of being, thereby expanding their definitions of themselves. They all, it seemed, had instinctively chosen the perfect roles for themselves. Thus the play—the rehearsals every bit as much as the final performance—became an important growth experience for all.

I'M GRADUALLY FINDING some peace in the belief that life itself is just plain metaphorical. The New Age paradigm known as the Gaia Hypothesis views the entire planet Earth as a living metaphor of sorts, leading me to conclude that each of us is free to create our own life-metaphors within this grand context, limited only by our own imaginations.

Practically speaking, we are all shaped and bounded by myriad influences, such as inherited traits, the attitudes of parents and society, and political and demographic realities. But the question I continue to raise is this: What real value does what we call education have if it is anything less than the means by which we each arrive at the fullest expression of ourselves for the limited time we have on this earth?

The late Joseph Campbell devoted his entire adult life to the study of myth and metaphor. I will always remember him for declaring the necessity of "following your bliss"—that is, unless you wanted to wake up one day late in life and sadly discover that "your ladder had been up against the wrong wall." At the Free School we try to resist the ever-present urge to race children through a series of academic hoops so that we can feel like successful teachers and at the same time quiet parents' fears that their kids aren't learning enough. We recognize the simple truth that no one else can find your bliss for you, because this is a process of self-discovery requiring an environment that supports such a task.

As I think Campbell would readily agree, children themselves are metaphors within metaphors, and their healthy growth demands a recognition of this vital dimension of human existence. Meanwhile, a problem I worry increasingly about is that young people today aren't so sure they even want to grow up. Part of the solution, I now know, lies in helping them discover that they have the power, with sufficient encouragement, guidance, and collaboration, to create a world worth living in.

8

Mr. Rogers

TV is chewing gum for the eyes.

—Frank Lloyd Wright

*O*ne day many years ago, we decided to go down and see if
we could get ourselves onto one of the big cargo ships that
periodically steam up the Hudson River to the Port of
Albany. There was a banana boat tied up at the dock that morning, and Rosalie managed to charm the captain of the enormous
ship into allowing us on board. Unfortunately, the district port
manager got wind of our plans and quickly brought them to a
screeching halt, claiming that insurance regulations prohibited
children from getting on the freighters. Not an unfriendly old
character, with a sympathetic, pouchy face, he could see how
crestfallen we were. Apologizing profusely, he offered us a tour of
the exterior of the banana boat from dockside, and we accepted.
He tried to interest the kids in various statistical data—height,
weight, length, draft, cruising speed—as we glumly stared up at
the ship, but the kids were just too disappointed to take much of it
in. Realizing, finally, that he was fast losing his audience, the
grandfatherly manager then did an amazing thing: He smiled a
beamy, weathered smile, summoned up his best radio
announcer's voice, and said, "Now boys and girls, do you want to
see an anchor?!?" The kids' response was like some ancient and
instinctive reflex. "Yay!!!" they screamed with sudden delight, and

we all went dashing toward the bow of the ship to see the anchor. Our guide patiently explained how the anchor worked, how much it weighed, and so on, and the children were absolutely entranced.

Meanwhile, I was dumbfounded. Since we take them out into "the real world" all the time, where they encounter adults and real-life situations of all kinds, Free School kids tend to be a bit more sophisticated than your garden-variety school group. I just couldn't believe how easily they had fallen for the old "Now, boys and girls . . ." routine.

And believe it or not, the entire scene replayed itself a few days later. A persistent Rosalie somehow managed to get the banana boat captain on the telephone and then work her magic on him a second time. He said that as far as he was concerned, we were most welcome on board his ship, that he would speak to the manager and clear it with him, and that we should come back down the next morning, which would be their last one in port.

This time it looked like we were in for sure. When we arrived, however, none other than the old manager was there to greet us again. Shaking his head, he told us that the well-meaning captain failed to understand that there were absolutely no exceptions to the Port of Albany's insurance regulations. He was sorry about the misunderstanding, and since we had gone to all that trouble to come down to the port again, he would be more than happy to let us walk alongside the ship one more time. We were all too dejected to refuse, and so we followed him, sheeplike, back down to the dock. When we reached the unloaded freighter, which was now sitting many feet higher in the water, our leader instantly changed his expression just like he had done the first time and once again intoned, "Now boys and girls, do you want to see an anchor?!?" I expected the apparently naive old guy to find himself with a small riot on his hands, maybe even discover himself suddenly in the river. Instead, just like before, a chorus of excited young voices cried out, "Yay!!" and once again the kids went dashing off toward the bow to see that same rusty old anchor still dangling down from its rusty old chain.

THIS STORY NAGGED at me for years until I gradually began to understand its meaning. Our old friend the port manager, whether he realized it or not, knew something that Mr. Rogers and every other kids' show host knows. Clowns and circus ringmasters know it, too. So does everyone in the advertising business. They recognize how enchantable children are and how nearly insatiable a need they have to move beyond the routine, mundane boundaries of day to day existence. This, of course, leaves them vulnerable to manipulation by the popular culture, and especially television.

The influence television exerts on children's emerging values, attitudes, and behavior has been the subject of much discussion—for good reason. These days there is almost universal agreement that the increasing prevalence of violence and pornography on TV is slow poison to American youth. And perhaps the ultimate insult is the manner in which the television and advertising industries exploit their soft spots. For instance, every morning they serve up rock 'em, sock 'em stuff, with scores of violent bits per thirty-minute segment, to little boys who are at the height of their aggressive-impulse formation. Next they flash extremely loud and irresistible advertisements for action figures at them every eight minutes. In my mind, this is tantamount to offering a thirsty alcoholic an ice-cold whiskey sour on a hot summer day.

Then there is the relatively new genre of programming aimed at teens and preteens where boy meets girl or girl meets boy and where all of the ads are for personal hygiene and body-image merchandise, thus taking full advantage of the great insecurity that most young people are experiencing at that age. This anything but subtle form of marketing literally works like a charm.

So why bring in Mr. Rogers here? His show has no sex or violence, nor are there any commercials. Furthermore, Mr. Rogers is a genuinely good person—an ordained minister, in fact—and he's using his show to teach positive values like caring and sharing, and lately, to help young children understand painful life issues like divorce. Thus, my apologies to him in the event that he ever reads this and is offended by my scapegoating him, as it were, in order to postulate the questionable side effects of even "good" television.

It's always a beautiful day in his neighborhood, as Mr. Rogers mesmerizes America's children day after day with his soothing voice and friendly smile. What can possibly be the harm in that? Just as Marshal McLuhan once said, the medium is, indeed, the message. And children's television is one very compelling medium. Again, no offense to Mr. Rogers, but suffice it to say that I will remain forever wary of the potential shows like his have for programming kids to rush off to look at anchors every time a kindly old man offers them the chance.

John Gatto astutely pointed out in an essay he once wrote about the hidden curriculum of schoolbooks that there are no longer any adults in the stories, only children existing in an artificial bubble—disconnected from parents, and from the past and the future as well. This kind of subtle mind control, says Gatto, plays a significant role in helping to train young people to become mindless cogs in the great consumer machine that feeds modern capitalism. Spend a Saturday morning watching children's programming and you will find the same to be true. These days the central cartoon figures are seldom even humanoid.

Contrast this with almost any fairy story, where the protagonist nearly always swears allegiance to family, past, and future. The beauty of these enduring tales is that each one offers a view of the entire cycle of life, containing elements of birth, childhood, initiation into adulthood, marriage, the pursuit of some kind of life ambition that almost always involves wounding, and ultimately, death. Cartoon heroes, on the other hand, escape unscathed week after week, and their brand of relentless aggression is delivered in a depersonalized package, wherein lies the greatest harm. The problem isn't only the frequency of the portrayal of aggression, it is the empty, inhuman context of the action, which stimulates children to treat each other in unfeeling and abusive ways.

In the ancient myths and fairy tales, it wasn't done this way at all. These timeless stories of human motivation and behavior reveal a psychology of earlier cultures that did not engender the kind of personal alienation that the youth culture is such an accurate barometer of today. The heroes of antiquity contained both good and evil that was plain for all to see. They didn't gently reason with witches, ogres, and dragons. Instead, they burned them up, or tricked them, or cut their heads off with sharp implements. And the stepsisters in Cinderella didn't come clean and confess to their deception; rather, the prince's messenger was tipped off by a sparrow and looked down to see the telltale blood still dripping from the glass slipper. In sum, those old tales of adventure and misadventure told the whole story of human existence— light side and dark.

Thanks to McCluhan's insight, we now know that television's subliminal message, whether it be of one-dimensional goodness or badness, only serves to make it more difficult for children to cope with the artificiality and confusion of modern life.

And then there is the addictiveness of television, regardless of the quality. According to Joseph Chilton Pearce, excessive television viewing is particularly harmful to the developing minds of young children, because it diminishes their capacity to create their own mental imagery. Image formation is a basic building block of intelligence and of the creative process, and it is what children ordinarily engage in when they read or are read to. Storytelling goes even one better because the medium, then, is entirely human and nonmanufactured and the listeners are always left to their own devices to color in the auditory outlines of the story. Television, on the other hand, provides children with ready-made images. If they watch too much, the area of the brain that performs this vital mental function can become lazy and even begin to atrophy.

Nowadays, because of the steady increase of television in many kids' diet of activity, I find that I have to work much harder at nursing them along when I read or tell them stories. I start with dramatic large-picture books and then progress to books with fewer and smaller pictures, then to books with no pictures. With any luck we eventually get to the point where I can simply tell them stories that succeed in holding their attention. Another trick I've learned over the years is to encourage kids to draw while I read or tell them stories. Actually creating their own physical images seems to help those who need it to bridge any imaginal gaps they may have.

Television is like a modern-day curse, which is not about to be willed, or wished, or its effects legislated, away. If anything, the arrival of the Internet, to which some experts claim 15 percent of American teenagers are already addicted, will only serve to lengthen the reach of television into children's minds.

Like any addiction, television is a symptom of a deeper disorder. All the children I know who watch too much do so because there's something missing in their lives. And this is because as a society we have managed to create a cultural vacuum—devoid of real challenge, real sensuality, real responsibility, and real meaning—that the television and entertainment industries have ever so successfully rushed in to fill. The seductive ease with which they have established themselves as substitutes for real living, and distractions from real concerns, is frightening indeed.

A FEW YEARS ago, a group of students (including Abby) put on a hilariously insightful skit at our end-of-the-year talent show, entitled "TV Sucks Your Brains Out." The dad in the skit is a closet TV addict who throws his kids outside one Saturday afternoon so he can sneak in a little television. But the kids catch on to the ploy and later in the day pull the very same trick on him. From all appearances, the skit is going to end with the kids mischievously watching away. What the audience doesn't realize is that under the kids' hats are surgical gloves filled with cooked spaghetti. A piece of monofilament fishing line is attached to them and stretches all the way to a hidden hand behind the make-believe TV set. Suddenly, the "brains" plop out onto the floor and are slowly sucked into the screen. This sight gag was so clever that three-quarters of the audience practically fell out of their chairs, they were laughing so hard.

Perhaps the best protection we can give kids is to help them understand the insidious nature of television. Generally we are only controlled by things when we are ignorant of their effects on us. Better still, we can help put kids in touch with enough compelling alternatives that the spell of television loosens its grip on them. That's why we try to expose Free Schoolers to so many different kinds of experience, and why we do all that we can to foster falling in love with one's interests.

Meanwhile, the only TV you'll find at the Free School at the moment is a hand-powered one. It was constructed by our six- and seven-year-olds, with a little help from Nancy. Actually, it's a cardboard box with a scrolling mechanism worked into it. The kids write and illustrate minidramas—with themselves as the stars, of course—on large scrolls, and then they carry the "set" up into the preschool to entertain the little kids, who are so delighted that they usually demand numerous encores. We're not antitelevision at all, we would just rather make our own.

9

God

THE MAGIC HAT

It began with a boy (as it so often does),
Bespectacled, wise, softhearted, and nine;
And a lone summer cap (one size fits all).
Of all the kids there, it caught his eye first . . .

Under the cap I had laid a brief note,
Hand-scribbled words claiming great promise:
This is *NO* ordinary hat; instead,
Lifelong happiness is its gift to the wearer.

The auctioneer held the hat high while he read:
"Booger Hollow, Arkansas, population seven—
(a most lucky number) *Countin' one coon dog.*
. . . *Who'll bid five dollars for this here hat?"*

A pudgy young hand shot straight up—it was Felix!
He'd watched me write that tantalizing note—
So this was no Frosty the Snowman routine;
No sleight of hand, storybook magic found here.

"Five dollars bid, five dollars, I'm lookin for six . . .
I've got six dollars bid, now how about seven?
Now seven, seven dollars, seven dollars, do I hear eight?"
Felix was far from the only believer.

(Magic makes believers, believers make magic.)
"Eight dollars bid, eight dollars, do I hear nine?"
. . . This hat is guaranteed to change your life.
"Nine dollars bid, nine dollars, I'm lookin for ten."

It was Felix again—he'd understood my refusal
When he asked for the secret.
The story of this hat is just for the winner.
"Ten dollars bid, ten dollars, who'll bid eleven?"

"I've got eleven dollars bid, now twelve, now thirteen . . ."
The bidding was fierce—for a tourist trap trinket?
Magic never appears in a businessman's ledger,
But forever lives on in free children's hearts.

"Fourteen dollars bid, I have fourteen, do I hear fifteen?"
No doubting Thomas, he just left his hand up now.
(But Felix means happy, so what's with the trick hat?)
It was a question of when and not why.

It was simply a matter of time now;
For Felix surely had come for the hat.
"Fifteen dollars, fifteen, fifteen, who'll bid sixteen dollars?
I've got sixteen dollars bid, sixteen, now how 'bout seventeen?"

(Sooner or later the others would realize.)
"I have a bid of eighteen dollars once, eighteen dollars twice . . .
Sold to the boy up front with the glasses."
(How had I known to bring him that hat?)

He paid his dues quick and came straight for my story.
I explained how the hat helped me through
And beyond my own cruel booger-man hollow;
Past cowardly demons 'till I reached my true self.

He tried on the hat and touched the bill softly.
"I've just got one question," he said, "but it's personal;
And so it's o.k. if you don't want to answer . . .
Can I ask what you paid for the hat?"

"Sure," I replied, "Just four dollars," and he smiled his eyes;
For he knew a real deal when he saw one.
Finally, Felix stood quite straight and quite tall,
And walked out into the dark Ozark night.

I wrote this poem while we were returning home from one of our annual two-week trips that the older class takes every year. It describes the centerpiece of an unusual sequence of events that occurred while we were attending the annual conference of the National Coalition of Alternative Community Schools, of which the Free School is a member. The conference, to which participating schools and homeschoolers often bring their children, had been hosted that year by another member school in the wild heart of the Ozarks, and we had traveled there by train and rental van.

At the top of the Free School teachers' agenda for this particular conference was challenging the organization's current leadership at the general membership meeting. The leadership had been refusing to deal face-to-face with some festering internal dissension and the entire coalition was suffering as a result. The other teachers and I were quite anxious about how our challenge would be received. In order to break the tension while we were driving from the train station to the conference site, we started piecing together a silly and obnoxious skit intended to poke fun at the people we were about to confront. We told ourselves that if we didn't receive the hearing we had traveled all that way to get, we would exact our revenge by performing our naughty little play at the conference talent show, which was set to follow the membership meeting, scheduled at the end of the weeklong affair.

As I drove the van headlong into the Arkansas wilderness, the silliness reached a crescendo. Egged on by the kids, we got into a rash of "booger jokes"; you know, ones like: "You can pick your friends and you can pick your nose, but you can't pick your friend's nose." At that exact moment, I spotted a billboard that read, "Booger Hollow, 27 miles." I was so startled I practically drove off the road. Dr. Bernie Siegel, the shaved-head physician with a unique and deeply spiritual approach to catastrophic illness says, "Coincidence is God's way of remaining anonymous." You don't say.

This was one of those tourist-trap deals where there is a huge sign every two or three miles to insure that you get lured in, especially if you're traveling with kids. It sure worked on us. Inside the Booger Hollow General Store, which was really a rambling old souvenir and trinket shop, we received our initiation into Ozark humor, which is as cornball as cornball gets, and right on our level at the time. While the kids browsed for keepsakes, the adults realized that this was the perfect place to pick up the props and sight gags for our embryonic skit. I have a fondness for hats, and so my most precious purchase was a Booger Hollow baseball cap.

Booger Hollow, as it turned out, is a real place, first settled by whites back in the eighteenth century; local legend has it that this particular hollow, as the depressions between the ancient worn-down mountains are called, was once inhabited by mysterious and terrible "bogeymen."

We arrived at the conference in a significantly lighter mood, and during the first few awkward days, kept refining our skit, just in case. It began to look as though we might actually have to go through with it, because the aforementioned leadership group was having little to do with that rowdy, disaffected bunch from Albany. In fact, we were practically shunned.

I was not looking forward to the membership meeting, having tangled with this group before, never with much success. Although I was feeling anxious, angry, and not very hopeful, I still cared a lot about our coalition, in whose growth and development the Free School had played an instrumental role.

I had placed myself on the agenda, and turned out to be the last floor speaker. The wait was excruciating. I am not at all comfortable addressing large groups, even when there's no public confrontation involved. I prayed that I might soften my anger in order to be articulate and that I might be fully heard.

Much to the relief of all, I think, my prayers were answered in full. Instead of getting angry, I was able to convey my deep regret over the polarized state in which the organization now found itself. I was not only heard, but was met with similar expressions of concern from many of those present. An hour-long dialogue ensued, and as a result, years of sometimes nasty infighting were cleared up then and there.

There's more. Sandwiched between the meeting and the talent show— where we would not be performing, after all—was the annual auction to raise money toward the coalition's operating expenses. Members are asked to bring something interesting to sell off, usually resulting in a delightfully raucous event. The problem was, we had been so focused on making trouble that no one from the Free School had remembered to bring anything for the auction. After a brief internal deliberation, I decided to donate my new hat, partly in the spirit of sacrifice—I really loved that hat—and partly as a cosmic joke, since the hat had been a piece of my costume in the skit that never was.

The poem tells of the auctioning of the hat; but there's an important postscript: At the following year's conference, I saw Felix again, a year older and a hatless head taller. I immediately wondered if he still had the hat. When I asked him about it, I got a very unexpected answer in return. Felix shared with me that his father had died during the summer from a brain tumor and that he had given his dad the hat at the onset of the cancer. Felix told me that his dad had worn the hat to cover up his bald head, but that he didn't know what happened to the hat after he died.

Here was an opening for me to share with Felix that my father, too, had died of cancer when I was a boy. Seeing that his grief and pain were as deeply buried as mine had once been, and since I was practically a stranger to Felix, I didn't engage him for very long. But later, moved by the tragic news, I decided to give him my one remaining memento from the Ozarks—a T-shirt that had the same Booger Hollow inscription as the hat. When I wrapped it, I included a note saying that magic often works in mysterious ways, and that I felt very strongly that when Felix gave his dad the hat, it had surely helped to ease his father's pain until he could reach a place where there is no suffering.

And then I was left to ponder how it was that Felix and I had come to make such an uncanny connection in the first place.

I DON'T KNOW whether a sense of the divine is innate or not, but it sure seems like it is. Perhaps because young children live in such a magical world already, they simply take for granted the existence of a power, or a being, or an energy greater than themselves. Most kids' realities are full of angels, spirits, gods, demons, and all sorts of other nonordinary phenomena, as Piaget confirmed in his studies of the stages of child development.

Actually, I don't ever remember meeting a child who didn't believe in God in one form, or by one name or another. Even young children whose parents are generally nonreligious seem to have a very deep sense of the reality of a spiritual dimension funded by a divine source. In any event, it's particularly fascinating to talk about matters of the spirit with kids who haven't been fed a lot of preset beliefs.

I remember one little girl whose image of God was a small giraffe. She was half Jewish; one Hanukkah, her father helped her to make a wooden menorah in the shape of a giraffe. She would then proudly bring it into school each year for the kindling of the Hanukkah lights.

And there was another young girl, whose mother and father are both Muslim, who carefully explained to me one day that God is a woman with dark green hair, and that sometimes at night She would carry her up into the sky on Her broad wings. I was instantly reminded of another of George McDonald's classics, *At the Back of the North Wind*, where the author portrays God as a beautiful woman who flies about the earth with her long dark hair streaming out behind—an image this five-year-old student couldn't possibly have known anything about.

Václav Havel, the poet and spiritual leader of the Czech Revolution as well as Czechoslovakia's first postcommunist president, said in a speech given on July 4, 1994, outside Independence Hall in Philadelphia, that the world has entered into a period of transition, cultural blending, and upheaval, which he and others term "postmodernism." His image of the current state of affairs is that of a bedouin mounted on a camel. The bedouin is clad in traditional robes, under which he is wearing jeans, with a transistor radio in his hands and an ad for Coca-Cola on the camel's back. Havel also said that we are already leaving behind the technological age, which brought about such an amalgamation of diverse cultures, when reason was king and science believed the universe to be an objective reality that could be explained entirely in rational terms.

Unbeknown to most, continued Havel, modern science's blind faith in the capacity of the human intellect to know all has left humanity feeling utterly confused and disconnected. This is because the more data we gather about the world, the less we intuitively understand the meaning and the purpose of our being here in the first place.

Havel's bedouin symbol of what is now known as "multiculturalism" thus becomes a grand paradox. At the very moment that there is this merging of the exterior expressions of different cultures, any unifying inner principle that might bind human beings together is fast disappearing. Havel warned that the human race is in danger of extinction unless we can find a way to regain a deep sense of knowing that we humans aren't the center of the universe—though we are mysteriously related to its every aspect—and that there is an ultimate source of meaning that is far greater than all of the human creations of all time put together.

According to Havel, the future of human life on earth depends on our rediscovering the invisible thread connecting all living things. He calls this "transcendence," and believes that it has the potential for guiding humanity toward a more peaceful coexistence because it is a unifying principle that resides closer to human hearts than matters of commerce or political ideology. Ever mindful of his backdrop, Havel concluded his speech with a reference to the claim in the Declaration of Independence that the Creator grants everyone the right to liberty, but reminded his audience that we will never realize that promise if we forget the One who endowed us with it in the first place.

LIKE VÁCLAV HAVEL, and like the nineteenth-century transcendentalists who are in many ways our forebears, the Free School believes it is imperative that children today have the opportunity to encounter the transcendent dimensions of everyday life. While we generally refrain from "teaching" religion as such—though Mary has from time to time offered a course on the world's religions—we are always on the lookout for opportunities for kids to experience a sense of the divine, or of some higher power, or of a feeling of interrelatedness and interconnection. Choose the idiom you feel most comfortable with.

For instance, when Betsy was our kindergarten teacher, she initiated a tradition with the four- and five-year-olds, one that continues on without her today. It involves an unorthodox use of the New York State Museum, located just a few blocks up the hill from the school. Oddly enough, the rear exterior of this singularly ugly chunk of modern architecture has a medieval touch: Two massive, white concrete staircases spiral upward from a seldom-used plaza to the top floor of the building. Lord only knows what those deserted stairs are actually for—some sort of fire escape, I suppose—but Betsy and her kids decided at one point that a fire-breathing dragon lives at the top of them. They also decided that the dragon would answer the wish or the prayer of anyone brave enough to hand deliver it (in writing) to the dragon's doorstep. The depth of their requests is always quite profound, but they are highly confidential and therefore cannot be revealed here.

The trick, of course, is to attempt an ascent of the staircase only when the dragon is out for the day. This (hopefully) can be determined by the absence of any steam or smoke behind the museum. The catch is you have to go up alone, and as you can imagine, not everyone makes it all the way on the first try. There are about two dozen steps altogether, but it probably seems more like two hundred dozen to a small child facing a possible encounter with a fire-breathing dragon, even if it's supposed to be a benevolent one. When kids find they just don't have it in them to make it all the way on the first try, it's not seen as a failure of courage, but rather as something to wrestle with for as long as it takes to conquer their fear. Generally everyone makes it by the third or fourth attempt.

Another of our teachers, Paul, a searchingly spiritual man who went from teaching doctoral-level political geography to helping young children understand the contents of their own souls, used to like to take kids down to the banks of the nearby Hudson River for a simple ritual he had conjured up. Everyone would take a piece of driftwood, inscribe their own personal prayer, launch it into the current, and then watch it until it disappeared downstream. Paul was living a life of Thoreauvian simplicity at the time, trying to recover his sense of himself after a stressful career in academia, and this was one of his ways of teaching kids how to find their own answers by connecting with the natural world.

One of my favorite winter things to do, especially when I am working in the preschool, is to take the little ones up to the nineteenth-century Roman Catholic cathedral two blocks away. It is generally empty most weekdays, and almost always left unlocked so that people can come in off the street to visit and pray.

It is an absolutely spectacular piece of sacred Gothic architecture, and I bring them there not to indoctrinate them with Christian beliefs, but so that they can experience what I consider to be an important physical metaphor. We tell ourselves we are visiting "God's House." Since in any given year the Free School might be comprised of Jews, Moslems, Christians of every stripe,

Buddhists, Unitarians, pagans, spiritualists, animists, twelve steppers, secular humanists, and even an occasional atheist or agnostic, I try to remember to explain to the kids that "God" is just my personal choice as a name for the divine. Others might use Allah, or Buddha, or Creator, or Holy Spirit, or Higher Power, which is fine because in the end we're probably pretty much all talking about the same thing. After one mother objected to my calling a Catholic church God's House, I have since made a point of telling the kids that God has as many different houses as God has names and forms.

The validity of these visits is confirmed for me every time I witness the awe and the reverence that comes over the faces of our kids as they pass through those huge arching portals into the silence and the shadows within. One of my main reasons for introducing them to the construct of God's House is simply to help ground them in a sense that God has a beautiful and an important place in this world and in their lives. More and more of them these days tend not to be temple, mosque or churchgoers, so I feel this is an especially important exposure for these kids in particular.

Again, just as we don't have much of a prescribed or standardized curriculum for reading, math, and science, we don't have one for religion either. Matters of the spirit tend to arise more or less spontaneously during the course of daily school life. For example, whenever anyone comes in with news of a death or an illness in their families, including, of course, cherished pets, we always get together to pray. The prayers take many different forms so as not to exclude anyone's beliefs. One beautiful tradition that has developed over the years is the singing of the song "Dear Ones." The words go like this:

> Dear ones, dear ones;
> Can I tell you what I know;
> You have given me your treasures;
> And I love you so.

We sing this universal little song in a round, and its power is unmistakable.

Whenever someone we know is injured or ill, we light a candle in the center of our circle. Then we silently send healing thoughts, prayers, and images to aid that person with his or her recovery. Once, Mary's grandson fell to the sidewalk from the top of a very tall tree in front of his home and completely shattered his face, among other serious injuries. Mary came into school on several successive mornings and led us all in a guided visualization where we imagined the bones of the boy's face knitting back together and the skin returning to its previous condition. The doctors were flabbergasted at the speed of his recovery.

Whether or not our praying actually had anything to do with the rapid healing that occurred is, I think, beside the point. What was important was the affirmation of the invisible connection of caring for a young boy who didn't even attend our school and whom many of our kids did not even know. In the end, regardless of who actually did what for whom, we all got to feel we had somehow shared in Mary's grandson's process.

The Free School does, on the other hand, make a conscious and deliberate effort to honor the holy days of all of the many religions practiced by our students, parents, and teachers. These special times are scattered throughout the school year, and celebrating them in the various ways that we do continually infuses our little community with a joyous richness. They also provide us with a steady stream of occasions for the kind of multicultural sharing for which there is such a need today.

THE TRUTH OF the matter is that science has slowly become our state religion, and our system of compulsory public schooling the all too eager enforcer of its official doctrine. John Gatto claims that there has been a more or less conscious conspiracy to remove God from the nation's schools so that children's loyalties can be shifted to more materialistic concerns and the juggernaut of consumer capitalism can proceed unabated. As disturbing as Gatto's theory is, I find it hard to refute.

In any case, it is certain that over the past several centuries the paradigm of Western science has slowly and silently atomized our collective consciousness to the point where now the feeling of being alone in a crowd is commonplace. Thousands upon thousands of middle-class Americans rush daily to the self-help shelves of bookstores or to expensive workshops and therapists, driven by an inner sense of disconnection and emptiness.

Fortunately, the most recent scientific pronouncements are beginning to sound downright mystical. These days, a book written by an expert in quantum physics and one authored by a theologian discussing the mysteries of his or her wisdom tradition can be difficult to tell apart.

Václav Havel is right, I am sure: the development of a spiritual identity that includes a sense of being connected to something greater than oneself has become an absolute imperative as we bear down upon the twenty-first century. Our young people are shouting out that many of the timeworn models and methods of cultural transmission aren't cutting it for them in this fast-changing and increasingly rootless society. More than anything else, they need us to support them in their personal searches for meaning, and they need accurate information to base their choices on. They also need to meet up with messages of tolerance, ones that reinforce the idea that there is no one right way to express or experience the transcendental dimensions of existence.

10

Race and Class

... *Fivescore years ago, a great American, in whose symbolic shadow we stand today, signed the Emancipation Proclamation. This momentous decree came as a great beacon of hope to millions of Negro slaves who had been seared in the flames of withering injustice. It came as a joyous daybreak to end the long night of their captivity.*

But one hundred years later, the Negro is still not free; one hundred years later, the life of the Negro is still sadly crippled by the manacles of segregation and the chains of discrimination; one hundred years later, the Negro lives on a lonely island of poverty in the midst of a vast ocean of material prosperity; one hundred years later, the Negro is still languished in the corners of American society and finds himself in exile in his own land.

... Let us not seek to satisfy our thirst for freedom by drinking from the cup of bitterness and hatred. We must forever conduct our struggle on the high plain of dignity and discipline. We must not allow our creative protest to generate into physical violence. Again and again we must rise to the majestic heights of meeting physical force with soul

force; and the marvelous new militancy which has engulfed the Negro community must not lead us to a distrust of all white people. For many of our white brothers, as evidenced by their presence here today, have come to realize that their destiny is tied up with our destiny. And they have come to realize that their freedom is inextricably bound to our freedom. We cannot walk alone. And as we talk, we must make the pledge that we shall always march ahead. We cannot turn back.

. . . I say to you today, my friends, so even though we face the difficulties of today and tomorrow, I still have a dream. It is a dream deeply rooted in the American dream. I have a dream that one day this nation will rise up and live out the true meaning of its creed, "We hold these truths to be self-evident, that all men are created equal." I have a dream that one day on the red hills of Georgia, sons of former slaves and the sons of former slave owners will be able to sit down together at the table of brotherhood. I have a dream that one day even the state of Mississippi, a state sweltering with the heat of injustice, sweltering with the heat of oppression, will be transformed into an oasis of freedom and justice. I have a dream that my four little children will one day live in a nation where they will not be judged by the color of their skin, but by the content of their character.

I have a dream today!

I have a dream that one day "every valley shall be exalted and every hill and mountain shall be made low. The rough places will be made plain and the crooked places will be made straight, and the glory of the Lord shall be revealed, all flesh shall see it together."

. . . With this faith we shall be able to transform the jangling discords of our nation into a beautiful symphony of brotherhood. With this faith we will be able to work together, to pray together, to struggle together, to go to jail together, to stand up for freedom together, knowing that we will be free one day. And this will be the day. This will be the day when all of God's children will be able to sing with

new meaning, "My country 'tis of thee, sweet land of liberty, of thee I sing. Land where my fathers died, land of the pilgrim's pride, from every mountain side, let freedom ring." And if America is to be a great nation, this must become true.

. . . So let freedom ring from the prodigious hilltops of New Hampshire; let freedom ring from the mighty mountains of New York; let freedom ring from the heightening Alleghenies of Pennsylvania; let freedom ring from the snow-capped Rockies; let freedom ring from the curvaceous slopes of California. But not only that. Let freedom ring from Stone Mountain of Georgia; let freedom ring from Lookout Mountain of Tennessee; let freedom ring from every mountain and molehill of Mississippi. From every mountainside, let freedom ring.

And when this happens, and when we allow freedom to ring from every village and every hamlet, from every state and every city, we will be able to speed up that day when all God's children, black men and white men, Jews and gentiles, Protestants and Catholics, will be able to join hands and sing in the words of the old Negro spiritual, "Free at last. Free at last. Thank God Almighty, we are free at last."

—Dr. Martin Luther King Jr., August 28, 1963,
Lincoln Memorial, Washington, D.C.

*I*n May 1994, events were staged across the country to commemorate the fortieth anniversary of the historic *Brown v. Board of Education* ruling that "separate but equal" schools are a violation of the equal protection clause of the United States Constitution. Here is what I observed at one such symposium held here in Albany.

As one might have expected, the majority of those in attendance were African American professionals working in various areas of education and social work. There were also a number of former civil rights activists, state and local NAACP leaders, and a smattering of whites, who like me are involved in education in one way or another. Overriding all of the nostalgic reminiscing was a strong desire among those assembled to call into question just how much things have actually improved since 1954.

There appeared to be a distinct correlation between the class status of the participants and their assessment of the situation. Not surprisingly, the university presidents, professors, and other icons of the middle class tended to have a more optimistic outlook and to emphasize how far African Americans have come in the past forty years. On the other hand, those whose career status was lower or whose work was primarily with the inner-city poor continued to feel frustrated and angry because of their daily experience with the de facto segregation that lives on in spite of all of the government's attempts to solve the problem by means of the law.

One woman, however, who now teaches African American studies at the state university, captured my attention with her story of growing up in the Deep South. She had been raised in a medium-sized town in Mississippi that had no white residents at all, and her perspective on segregation was one I'd never heard expressed before in quite that way. Essentially, she said that the "segregation" she had experienced in her youth—perhaps racial isolation is a more apt term in this instance—had been entirely positive, because all of her important role models then—the mayor, the school principal and teachers, the doctors and nurses, the newspeople, the artists, the entertainers, and so on, were African Americans just like herself.

Thus, this woman in no way felt damaged or deprived by her past—in fact, she saw it as quite the opposite. Her presentation at the symposium served to round out the spectrum of perspectives, and to remind me that the issue of racism is another extremely complex one. Still, the variety of viewpoints notwithstanding, the consensus of this two-day gathering was that the promise of the *Brown* decision, of ending the condition whereby nonwhite children are condemned to a separate and unequal education, remains unfulfilled.

ANY EXAMINATION OF the state of education in America that ignores the converging political and economic realities of race and class is sure to be shallow and self-serving, contributing only to the denial upon which the problem of fundamental inequality depends for its continued existence.

Discussions about racism all too often fail to include social class. It was for this reason that I left the two-day *Brown* symposium with lingering misgivings. Certainly the sole focus there had been on racial issues, with a glaring omission of any in-depth look at the relationship between social class status and "educational opportunity" in this so-called democracy of ours. Perhaps this was a fundamental shortcoming of the Warren Court's original analysis, one that has ended up contributing to the lack of any real change over the last four decades.

It's no secret that the defense of the class system has always been a primary goal of the capitalist economic model, with racism merely being one among many effective means toward that end. It's also no secret that this nation-state of ours was founded by a group of men who were, among other things, determined European American, middle-class opportunists, and that later the battle over slavery also would have, at its core, the issue of economics.

However, a fact that appears to be a lot less well known is that in the post–Civil War era, the agenda of the founding fathers of our current system of compulsory, government-controlled schools was, above all, to protect their own economic interests in the face of the sweeping demographic changes brought on by the industrial revolution. Some, like the Carnegies and the DuPonts, would be most forthright about their goal of establishing a hierarchical structure, with the cream of the crop running the show and the rest operating the machinery. Their successors have since done a brilliant job of covering up the true intent of the system with euphemistic phrases like "equal opportunity" and social programs like "Head Start."

Perhaps no one better understands the economic roots and the institutionalization of racism reinforced by the public schools better than Jonathan Kozol. In a recent book, he spells out the dynamics of race and class in our nation's schools, which he summed up in the title *Savage Inequalities.*

As Kozol so graphically confirms, the situation isn't getting better, it's getting worse. The number of six-year-old children in America living in poverty has risen 20 percent in the past five years and is now more than one in four. Meanwhile, the world's 286 billionaires now control approximately half of the wealth on the planet. What this means at the level of our public schools is that the rich districts will continue to get richer and the poor ones poorer, insuring the game will remained rigged.

And conditions in our inner cities are hardly improving. The economic racism refined to such a high art during the Reagan/Bush years, which is now producing unemployment rates as high as 60 and 70 percent among young urban black males, remains unaddressed.

These economic realities all but guarantee that racism will remain alive and well for the remainder of this century and into the next. A distinct color line will continue to run through all of our major social institutions—educational, medical, financial, legal, and judicial. Increasingly segregated housing patterns will continue to confound urban school systems throughout the nation as they flail away at the persistent problem of segregation.

The plain truth, one kept well hidden by careful political image management, is that racial and economic prejudice proliferate at the center of our culture.

THE RIDDLE "HOW DO YOU EAT AN ELEPHANT?" comes to mind. The answer, of course, is "One bite at a time." When Mary started the Free School she decided to take Jonathan Kozol up on the challenge he had issued in a much earlier book, *Free Schools,* and locate her experiment in the heart of the inner city. She was determined that the poor of all races would have ready access to a school that would endeavor to meet the multilevel needs of their children.

This meant, especially in the early days, that the school played a role not unlike that of nineteenth-century settlement houses like Jane Addams's Hull House in Chicago. We provided transportation to those who needed it; we started a free breakfast and lunch program so that kids would be assured of two complete meals a day; we distributed used clothing; we found English tutors for Puerto Rican immigrants; we even helped families finance and rehabilitate their own homes. Kids came—and still come—to school by day and on occasional evenings we hold potluck suppers and fund-raising dinners, or invite speakers in to address issues of common concern such as nonabusive ways to discipline children, children and divorce, and the effects of television. Our efforts have helped to stabilize all four sides of an entire city block.

But then, as now, the external dimensions of race and class prejudice are in many ways easier to remedy than the internal, nonphysical ones. This isn't to say that dealing with the physical effects of poverty on families isn't a constant challenge; but what is to be done about the way it eats away at a child's soul like a cancer, especially when racism is a factor?

Chief Justice Earl Warren understood the depth of the problem implicitly when he wrote in the majority opinion for the *Brown* decision: "Segregated schools generate a feeling of inferiority as to children's status in the community . . . unlikely ever to be undone." Then there is the field research of Dr. Robert Coles. Coles, a distinguished child psychiatrist at Harvard who for decades has been reporting on the impact of poverty and racism on children's psychological development, continues to find in his work with ghetto children not far from Harvard's ivy-covered walls that feelings of inferiority in black children in particular are as prevalent as ever.

At the Free School we try to address the internalized effects of racism in many ways, some direct, some indirect. Probably the most obvious response is to study and honor the lives of African American heroes and leaders, to fill in the gaps left in the standard American history texts used in most schools. We do as much of this as we possibly can. Most years our kids will stage a play about Dr. Martin Luther King Jr. and the civil rights movement around the time of Dr. King's birthday. Also, we once joined a Japanese Buddhist group that was retracing the path of the Underground Railroad in New York State. As part of that unforgettable three-day experience, the kids got to tour the house where Harriet Tubman lived in Auburn and to visit her gravesite nearby.

When history is brought to life in this way, children receive the full restorative impact of its messages of heroism, pride, and accomplishment. Also, the value of compelling role models cannot be overstated. For example, each of the boys I have seen play the role of Dr. King in our school productions over the years underwent a personal transformation in the process. They were all vulnerable kids from struggling families, and yet they all have grown into competent, respectable young men, each of them a potential leader with a real understanding of racial and economic justice.

When our kids stage their plays on the life of Dr. King, they usually include a scene, based on the story found in the popular King biographies written for children, where young Martin is playing with a white friend down the street from his boyhood home in Atlanta. Suddenly the white boy's mother leans out her door, shoos Martin away, and then says to her son something like, "You know I don't want you around *his* kind. Now get in this house right now." Young Martin runs home to his mother, who explains to her perplexed son the state of race relations in the 1930s. She concludes with the consoling words: "Martin, no matter what happens to you in this world, you've always got to remember one thing—you are *somebody*."

Engendering a sense of "somebodiness" is perhaps the best thing we do in our school to reverse the side effects of race and class prejudice. In an environment where everyone is viewed as someone special, where everyone gets a chance to lead, and where everyone is free to set one's own challenges and to pursue one's own genius, children with damaged self-images often recover a positive, confident sense of themselves very quickly.

In an atmosphere of genuine, as opposed to theoretical, equality and democracy, the symptomatic expressions of prejudice—the inward-directed feelings of worthlessness and the outward expression of superior hostility—have so little function or relevance that they simply atrophy from lack of practical application. In other words, if a group of children knows it truly has an equal stake in the situation, and if their footing is equal as well—always the case in our school—then it is very difficult for prejudice to take root, at least for very long.

In spite of the fact that any number of our kids—from either side of the equation—have race and class prejudice in their backgrounds, you will seldom find those negative attitudes coloring their daily interactions in school. And this is not because they are suppressed, but because prejudice, being rooted in fear and ignorance of others different from oneself, is hard to maintain when kids of all races and social classes are working and playing joyfully together side by side.

All of this isn't to say that prejudice doesn't rear its ugly head in our school from time to time—it does. And when it does we simply try to meet it head-on. Nothing fancy, no curriculum niceties, no sensitivity training for the staff; we just talk about what happened and try to get at the truth. We look for answers to basic questions like: "Why did you call so and so a such and such?" "What did you mean by that and why do you believe it?" "How would you feel if someone treated you that way?" When children aren't being judged or punished for their beliefs and actions, they are usually perceptive and forthright, and quite willing to let go of antisocial attitudes. Any number of lifelong interracial friendships began in our little school.

And yet, it doesn't always go so smoothly. For instance, years ago we had taken an African American single mother and her three young children under our wing. They had recently migrated to Albany from the South, arriving with little more than the clothes on their backs. The oldest boy, James, who was about eight at the time, became very attached to me, and vice versa. One day, Robin, an older girl, feisty and outspoken, from a working-class white ghetto family, got angry with James—about what, I can't remember—and shouted at him, "You stupid little nigger!" Standing right there, I saw the look of deep shame come over James's face. Without thinking, and before I could register just how angry I was, my hand left my side to slap Robin. Fortunately, we were able to resolve the situation without any permanent damage being done. Robin and her family weren't unfamiliar with rough-and-ready forms of adult "discipline," and my apology and assurance that I would never do something like that again were met with a similar response from both Robin and her mother.

Thus far we haven't perfected any formulas for curing race and class prejudice, and I suspect we never will. We try different things at different times and usually we proceed more appropriately than in the preceding example. The key at all times is the awareness that prejudice is always going to be a piece in the puzzle of human interaction. It is virtually impossible, I think, to grow up in this world without acquiring prejudice in one form or another, and often we simply are not aware that it is an active ingredient in our actions or reactions toward another person.

Teachers certainly are not immune from this reality. We carry prejudice within us, too; usually in subtler forms than the kids, because we know it's wrong. Again, awareness and open communication are the answer. For instance, when one or more of us finds ourselves disliking or disapproving of a particular child, we are careful to ask ourselves whether or not prejudice of some sort might be a factor in our attitudes. When it is, we try to bring our prejudices to the surface and then let them go so that they don't dictate our responses to the children, many of whom are vulnerable to being influenced simply by how we feel about them.

Race and class prejudice are not hopeless problems, as long as they are kept out in the open and not stuffed away into some dark closet and allowed to fester and multiply. At least this is true in a school the size of ours, where the elephant *can* be eaten a bite at a time.

I SUSPECT I will always share Dr. King's dream that one day all God's children will be able to sit at the table together. And I am convinced that the most direct route to fulfilling it is to bring together children of all kinds in environments—and not necessarily school ones—free of external ranking and competition where they can discover how to share their common interests as well as understand and respect their differences. Tolerance cannot be taught, nor can it be learned from a textbook.

But my optimism fades whenever I look out at the bigger picture. Socially engineered mass-solutions like forced busing have been tried, and almost all have failed to bring about any real and lasting change. As long as we continue to ignore the economic dimensions of racism, this will continue to be so. In the meantime, the human costs of the unanswered dilemma of race and class in this country are incalculable, and Dr. King's dream will remain just that—*a dream.*

11

Sexuality

HALLOWEEN

lipstick red leather
size eleven
double width
not built for comfort
or for speed
(don't try to run
honey)

out of the box
they stand like
twin ski jumps
inclined
to throw me
up out of my
closet

night vehicles
idling nervously
my pulse races
as I slip them on
like red corvettes
(honey don't set
the cruise control)

everal autumns ago, I was working primarily with the school's oldest kids, who happened that year to range in age from about ten to twelve. This meant the majority of them were pacing right on the threshold of that raucous developmental stage we call adolescence. Along came three eleven-year-old boys—practically simultaneously—all of whom had just bailed out of their neighborhood public schools. Predictably, our three young musketeers thought they were pretty hot stuff and that our strange little school was ripe for the picking—especially the girls in their new class.

Now these weren't bad kids by any means; if we could have taken them on one at a time, I'm sure each of the boys would've relaxed more quickly into the flow of the school. But their proximate arrival became the basis of a bond that wasn't likely to be broken any time soon. And so, while this trio of preteen ne'er-do-wells was busy trying to establish a school unto themselves, constantly testing to see how far they could stretch the limits, I was left to ponder how to get their attention and perhaps change their channel a little bit, at least one to the right or left on the dial.

This proved to be no small challenge, since these boys already had years of training in guerilla acts of resistance and rebellion under their respective belts. To top it all off, they no longer appeared to have any respect whatsoever for females—the gender of most, if not all, of their previous teachers—and only accorded me a grudging deference based on the fact that I was a more powerful male whom they perceived as (sort of) in charge.

My inspiration came just before Halloween, which the Free School has always taken very seriously. I had my wardrobe, two makeup artists (my wife and a sixteen-year-old former student with bags full of cosmetics) and a borrowed electric beard trimmer all ready and waiting for me. Right in the middle of the big day, I snuck out of school and dashed home to change. I shaved as close to my face as I possibly could without taking off any skin and then my pit crew quickly and hilariously began to transform me. One applied layer after layer of face and eye makeup while the other teased and curled my shoulder-length hair. Then they packed me into one of Betsy's slinkiest dresses and off I rushed to school, heels in hand.

When I strutted back into our classroom less than an hour later on my three-inch red leather pumps (the subject of the above poem), no one—and I mean no one—recognized me. I entered without saying a word, leaned up against one of the vacant desks, and began smiling at you-know-who. They, just as I had hoped, could not take their eyes off me. About as subtly as a three-alarm fire, they looked me over from head to toe and back again. I waited until I couldn't stand the suspense any longer and then said to them in my own natural tenor, "What do you think you're looking at, *boys?*"

Words can't do justice to the ensuing madness. If faces can fall off, then that is precisely what happened to my three junior gangsters. Like the Three Stooges, they fought to be first through the door. All three ran straight out of the building, one screaming, "It's Chris!!!" another moaning, "My teacher is a faggot," and the third simply muttering to himself over and over, "Oh, my God. Oh my God." It must have been twenty minutes before they would even come back inside the school again. In the meantime, the girls and I enjoyed the laugh of a lifetime.

The rest of the afternoon, needless to say, was a real corker. I tried to remain in character as much as possible and had a ball playing around on the other side of the gender line. The following day, and for several days after that, none of the three boys could even begin to look me in the eye without falling apart all over again. Things then slowly returned to normal, if there is such a thing in our school, and while I can't claim that my little adventure in cross-dressing had brought about any immediate results, I had found the edge with them that I had been searching for.

THE DELICATE, PERSONAL and controversial subject of sexuality is almost never sufficiently discussed in conjunction with children. It's just too hot a topic. But you're perhaps wondering what this opening story has to do with sexuality. I believe it has a great deal to do with the attitudes and behaviors that had gotten the targets of my practical joke in such trouble in their previous schools and that were fast heading them toward disaster even in our unconventional setting. In short, their accumulated prejudice against females and generalized disrespect for anything other than themselves, as well as their rapidly growing cockiness, all had a strong sexual component.

With these boys just peeking through the door of adolescence, I knew it wasn't too late for them to change. I also knew that dealing with them in the standard authoritarian, moralistic way they were already so inured to was not about to have the least effect. My little dose of shock treatment was simply to get their attention. I was opening up the issue of sexuality in a totally unexpected way, and at the same time, I was acknowledging playfully—yet with a seriousness that would come out in later discussions—the obvious fact that they were fast becoming sexual young men. And somehow, in so doing I immediately earned their respect.

Not surprisingly, the first thing the boys came back at me with in the days following was their rampant homophobia. How could a man ever do such a thing (this was long before the release of a series of very well-received box office hits on the subject)? Did it mean I was gay? Suddenly we found ourselves in a whole-class debate about just what it is to be gay. Is it bad or wrong? Is it okay for some, but not for others? Is it even something that should be openly discussed?

The girls were infinitely more relaxed about the subject. Several of them were willing to share that they have gay friends or relatives, which immediately brought down the boys' level of homophobia a notch—I suspect because the same was true for them. I was able to raise the question of why it tends to be so much more difficult for boys to talk about this issue, which led to a thoughtful examination of the widespread prejudice against homosexuals in our society. I asked the boys to look at whether fear might not be at the root of male macho sexual attitudes. And just to make sure we were on the same page, I reminded them of how aware I was of the way they had undressed me with their eyes on Halloween. They grinned at me sheepishly and agreed that machismo is often a cover for underlying insecurity.

This brought us to exactly where I had hoped we would arrive—back at the crucial issue of respect. As though a floodgate had been opened, the girls began telling the boys how disrespected they felt by their vulgarity and their explicit sexual references. They demanded and received assurances from the boys that they would stop. I pointed out how much generalized contempt for women persists in our culture and then I praised the boys to the skies for their willingness to let in what the girls had to say. I also thanked the girls for their forthrightness. And I took full advantage of the opportunity to point out that this was a perfect example of the difference between male bravado and real courage.

The three boys didn't change overnight, nor did they ever entirely leave behind their old ways. But their attitude toward the girls and the women teachers improved gradually with time, and when they reentered public school over the course of the following year, each was able to make a successful transition.

I GUESS THE official name for the preceding group discussion, which actually turned out to be a series of informal conversations, is what is known today as sex education—that cold, dead fish wrapped in three-week-old newspaper, under whose banner our schools supposedly attempt to teach kids what they need to know about sex but are afraid to ask. Now don't get me wrong; at least it demonstrates the school system's audacity to use the word (*sex*) openly. The trouble is, the schools so often approach the subject in a sterile, lifeless, nonrelational fashion.

Debates rage on about how much information about sex is appropriate for young people. A local example: Not long ago, the New York State Education Department published a teachers' manual about the HIV virus. The first edition was excellent. It carefully explored adolescent sexual attitudes and patterns of behavior, gave a solid, scientific explanation of HIV/AIDS and how it is and isn't transmitted, and then provided a comprehensive section on safe sex practices. However, following a violently negative reaction from conservative groups across the state, the booklet was recalled and ordered destroyed (I kept mine). A "sanitized" version was later reissued, which preached abstinence ad nauseam.

My own firm conviction is that there is no such thing as giving adolescents too much information about their emergent sexuality, because kids want and need to know the facts. I do not believe that knowing about sex in and of itself is dangerous, that it leads to experimentation and unsafe behavior. In spite of the airtime abstinence is getting these days, increasing numbers of American teenagers are sexually active. This says to me that every question about sexuality that goes without an accurate, honest, caring answer is an accident waiting to happen somewhere.

The question of timing is another matter altogether. I can entirely understand the fear of some parents that their kids will be exposed to information about sex before they are ready. Children mature at different rates, and it can be very damaging to a child's evolving sense of self if sexual information is forced on them too soon, or without their being able to discuss their accompanying fears and confusion. This issue, perhaps as well as any, serves to highlight the utter fallacy—and sometimes the outright harm—in herding children together in cramped, age-segregated rooms and insisting that they consume a standardized curriculum.

CERTAIN YEARS AT the Free School the subject of sexuality comes up piecemeal, as in the one I described above, and other years the older kids will ask for a regular class—usually in the spring, of course. Mary used to lead a great sex-ed class, and now sometimes Betsy, who is still our school nurse, and I will coteach one. When we do, we always have a lot of fun with it.

We usually begin by establishing a few simple ground rules: no one has to attend if they don't want to (the kids always seem to be able to sort out for themselves who's ready and who isn't—and there is no stigma whatsoever attached to not participating), no questions barred, absolutely no teasing or put-downs, and complete confidentiality outside of our weekly sessions.

There is no lesson plan to be found here. The kids' excellent, sometimes challenging questions provide the jumping-off point for some very deep and provocative discussions. For example, sexually transmitted disease is a huge concern for them these days, as well it should be. The year that Jesse was in the class, he shared that several of his mother's old friends either had AIDS or had already died from it, and he asked if that was the case for anyone else. This led to an exploration of loss, death, and dying—another critically important topic our schools, which only mirror the larger society, also tend to avoid if they can.

I am always shocked when I hear from the boys how much pornography they have been exposed to via cable television and videos. Such material has a disastrous impact on their attitudes toward females. Telling them not to watch this poison would accomplish little at this late date; so instead, we talk about what it is these movies are communicating and why they watch them. The girls jump right into the discussions, which then heat up in a hurry, providing the boys with feedback I could never give them.

Counteracting society's prevailing tendency to denigrate women is a daunting task to say the least, and all I can think to do is to keep pulling the boys back to the fact that true sexuality is a mutual exchange of caring and desire between two people, and that it is certainly the most satisfying when it occurs within a relationship that is grounded in tenderness and respect. I look for openings to say to them that there is also a sacred dimension to joining with another person in a sexual way, and whenever possible I introduce language that expresses lovingness and beauty rather than the hostility and self-gratification that they hear over and over again on the "X-rated" channels.

If straight information is what the kids want, Betsy and I give it to them just that way, though usually not unless they ask and never if they show signs they are becoming overloaded. Generally, they really want to know what's what; so we hold nothing back because we believe that kids have both a right and a need to know.

But far more important than whatever information that might or might not be exchanged in our class is the modeling that Betsy and I do for the kids. They are as intent on *who* and *how* as on *what* we are saying. This is true with any subject, and it especially applies to sexuality. When education around sexual issues is reduced to data and cautionary propaganda, it is as lifeless and irrelevant as the term "sex education" sounds.

Betsy and I aren't afraid to get personal with the kids. They always seem to appreciate our willingness to share recollections of our own awkward adolescent moments, or how we fell in love, or what we do when we find we aren't getting along very well. I remember one year when the oldest boy in the class, who was already sexually active at fourteen, held back from contributing anything to the discussions until I shared my friend's hilarious story about his initial unsuccessful attempt to put on a condom for the first time.

The most important message Betsy and I try to get across is that sexuality is at the same time a delicate, precious energy and a potent, spellbinding force that can be either creative or destructive. We don't shy away from expressing our own often strong opinions about certain rights and wrongs and dos and don'ts, and we stress that sexuality is most safely and happily shared within the context of a loving relationship. Above all else, we remind them how crucial it is for them to learn to remain aware of and to trust their own feelings and instincts—about themselves, the other person, and the situation.

HERE IS THE place to finish telling about Allan, our legendary birdman. I left off with him attending his local public middle school, and doing quite well. By the end of that year, he decided he had had enough of the once-removed learning that constitutes our national curriculum. He had proved to himself, his parents, and the world—once and for all—that he could do it, and now he was eager to move onto something more compelling and interesting. So clear was his desire that he managed to gain entrance, along with a substantial scholarship, to a residential alternative school located in an abandoned Shaker community in western Massachusetts. The school in some ways operates according to the Shaker model, which values the centrality of purposeful work. By his fourth year, Allan was the head of the entire student body. He graduated with several awards and is currently pursuing a career in the military.

Meanwhile, during his senior year in high school, Allan wrote an essay about his Free School experience for *ΣΚΟΛΕ, the Journal of Alternative Education*. He began by describing how much he had come to hate school and anything that had previously fit under the heading of "learning." For him, the Free School became not only a place where he gradually came to love learning, but where he also *learned to love* (emphasis his). Such a profound statement from the hand of a seventeen-year-old male in this society!

Allan went on to explain how this learning had come about. Affecting him most deeply was the fact that both the other students and the teachers in the school had cared about him exactly as he was, warts and all. He always knew that he was respected and valued for simply being himself, that he was listened to and given consideration for *his* thoughts and *his* ideas, and that sometimes he was able to teach the adults in return. What restored his desire to learn and grow, he concluded, was the intimacy he had shared with other students and teachers during his time with us.

LOVE, RESPECT, INTIMACY, CARING—aren't these the basic ingredients of a healthy sexuality, broadly defined?

Carl Jung viewed sexuality as a boundless force that transcends the physical to encompass the realms of human creativity and spirituality. And that is why, in our school, we try never to restrict "sex education" to a classroom subject, even though it sometimes becomes one for our adolescent students. As I think Allan is trying to say, sexuality as loving/caring/intimacy/respect is an everyday part of our school life.

Our working definition of sexuality, like Jung's, is also very broad. For instance, we always try to give the needs of the body their full due. The school environment is filled with physicality: running, riding, jumping, tumbling, wrestling, dancing, singing, dressing up, painting, throwing pots on the wheel, playing the piano, chasing, playing four-square, and so on. Creativity and imagination are celebrated at all times. We watch for signs of damaged self-image or body-shame because these kinds of negativity are a heavy burden for a child to carry through life. It is the lack of fundamental self-respect, as much as anything else, that leads young people to make poor or unsafe life choices. In the end, we equate sexuality with aliveness, or what Henri Bergson called the elan vital, and we look for every available opportunity to nurture its growth in all of its many facets.

While there remains much disagreement around the moral and psychological dimensions of adolescent sexuality in particular, few, I think, would argue against the importance of helping children to develop a model of sexuality that is founded on love, responsibility, caring, and commitment to others. That perhaps is what we do best of all through our continual emphasis on the primacy of human relationships.

As George Dennison was courageous enough to repeat again and again in his precious book, *The Lives of Children*, love is one of the fundamental reasons for our being on this earth. The logic behind this statement, as far as education is concerned, is almost too simple to merit elaboration: Love engenders happiness, and happy children will learn all the skills, facts, and concepts they need to make their way in this world far more quickly and far more easily than unhappy ones.

This makes the individual effort to develop the wherewithal to give and receive love the most fundamental of all learning tasks, and therefore should place it at the top of the list of priorities of everyone in America interested in the healthy education of our children.

12

Teaching

Man is born like a garden ready planted and sown.

—William Blake

*E*very so often, Missy, who directs the preschool now, gets out her easel and her sketchbook and sets up shop in a quiet corner of one of the downstairs classrooms. She closes the door, rigs up a good, bright light next to the subject's stool, sharpens up her set of artist pencils and voilà: an instant portrait studio.

Before long kids are clamoring to have Missy draw them; sometimes it takes a solid week or more for her to get everyone in. Usually I or another downstairs teacher will take her place upstairs so that she can stay in her studio and gradually work her way through the line of eager young models.

What Missy doesn't tell the kids is that this is her art class. She is showing them how to draw.

The teaching process begins with Missy's own feeling for her craft. She loves doing portraits and her joy quickly expands to fill the room. For her subjects, the experience of being drawn, of watching their own image slowly appear on Missy's easel, is enthralling. It's like seeing a photograph magically materialize in a darkroom developing pan.

Missy is careful to position herself so that the kids have a clear view of her as she draws. Probably without even realizing, they are watching her motions and mannerisms intently. A little like a chatty hairdresser, Missy keeps up a light banter to quell impatience and prevent the atmosphere from getting too serious. She points out to each subject the items of distinction in their features as she draws them, describes her movements with the pencil, and alternately remains quiet as she sketches away with great concentration.

Just like artists in Central Park, Missy attracts a crowd while she works. Her enjoyment is contagious. She doesn't mind the gang of kids gathered around to watch, because she knows that just like her subject, the onlookers are intently studying her technique.

On the second or third day of the run, you'll find Missy seated on the subject's stool. Her former subject is now her student and she might, if the mood is right, begin to give some light instruction. How much directed teaching she will do will depend on the needs and wishes of each individual child, and on the chemistry between student and teacher.

Before it's all over, the room will be full of kids drawing other kids, or drawing themselves, and Missy will be floating around answering questions and giving encouragement. The portrait light—now lights—will stay on continuously. A display wall will quickly fill with art work of extraordinary quality. And the drawings won't be coming from a handpicked group of precocious young artists but from whoever decided to hang around and try it out for themselves. Always most impressive to me are the sketches done by kids who don't necessarily have a gift for portraiture. Their leap in skill during that single week with Missy is nothing short of remarkable.

The class ends when there aren't any more portraits to be drawn. There's no art show and no prizes. Missy simply thanks everybody for a great time, packs up her things, and goes back upstairs to her little ones.

MANY MIGHT THINK a loose and open-ended approach to teaching is fine in areas like art, but what about hard-core skills areas like reading, writing, and arithmetic? Or science or history? Don't they require more rigor and regimen?

The answer, I think, is an unqualified maybe. Or a hearty it all depends. But certainly not necessarily, as the nation's curriculum experts would have us all believe. For instance, when Nancy is teaching reading, oftentimes she just reads aloud to her students. She selects good, compelling stuff, or the kids bring in favorite selections of their own. And just as Missy draws, Nancy reads with excitement and passion. Kids gather round close to her and she changes expressions and voices to bring the characters to life right there in the room. There's no time limit either; she usually doesn't stop until everyone's too tired to listen any more.

Sometimes Nancy mixes in instruction. She teaches phonics, gets students to read along with her, writes down their stories and has them read them back, encourages them to create their own newspapers and magazines. It was Nancy who helped the kids make that hand-powered "television" I referred to earlier, which told each episode in subtitles. Without a whole lot of fanfare she posts their stories and poems on the walls, and helps each of them to maintain an active file of their work on the classroom Macintosh. And Nancy never forgets that play is a huge component of the learning process. She doesn't want the kids to think of reading as hard work.

Meanwhile, dozens of young children learn to read under her auspices without necessarily having been "taught." Some kids need a lot of help learning to read, others little or none at all. Woody, who has been teaching reading for more than fifty years at the Peninsula School, one of the nation's longest-running alternative schools, states emphatically that there are as many ways to teach reading as there are students to learn. It is imperative, she says, for a teacher to respect the individuality of every student, to help them find, in her words, "the magic way" that works for them.

Mary preferred a mythological approach to teaching. One year, for example, she and a group of kids invented a magical adventure game against which the more recent "Dungeons and Dragons" would pale by comparison. Dubbed "The Cellar Adventure," the game was very Tolkienesque and involved hunting buried treasure in a mysterious land filled with ogres and dragons. First, they wrote out the game's rules, characters, and story line, and even created maps. Then they spent a great many days enacting the drama in real life. Suddenly the school's dark, dirt-floored cellar—accessible only by a heavy trap door—became its most popular and exciting classroom.

The game involved reading and writing, but that's not really why Mary cooked it up. She was operating according to her keen awareness that awakened and engaged children learn better. She also understood the almost limitless power inherent in a group process where, when it is a mutually supportive one, everyone brings out the best in each other. So her first order of business every year was to help kids form real working teams; then as time passed, to stop whenever necessary to repair any tears in the fabric that might have occurred along the way. No one ever got left behind, and whenever someone would begin to drift away, she would turn it over to the rest of the group to bring the odd child out back into the circle. The kids responded magnificently to the challenge of this level of responsibility, in part, I surmise, because it galvanized in them a feeling that it was *their* class, and not just Mary's.

What always amazed me the most about Mary's teaching style was her indomitable belief in every student's ability to succeed. She absolutely refused to give up on anyone. Once, before she started the Free School, while still teaching at a small private school in then-segregated Texas in the early 1960s, she took under her wing a black high school student who was struggling academically. Even though the young man wasn't keeping up in his standard subjects, he elected to join Mary's Latin class. He then proceeded not only to become accomplished in that classical language, but to transfer the model of competence he had internalized there to other areas—to such an extent that he was able to go on to college and then to a successful professional career. Now, he writes to Mary each Christmas to fill her in on the latest news of his life and to thank her for the difference she made in it. Mary would be the first to say that her former student deserves all the credit for his amazing turnaround, and of course that is so. Nevertheless, the power of the role of teacher, properly played, must never be overlooked.

JOHN GATTO WRITES in *The Empty Child:* "Kids don't resist learning; they resist teaching." A few years earlier, Herb Kohl wrote an entire book with the very same thesis. Called *I Won't Learn From You,* it explores the tremendous damage done to children in our schools by negative teaching. Just as the title suggests, Kohl says that the poor performance of a great many students is often not due to any shortcoming on their part. Rather it is an expression of their will to resist the control of adults who they feel do not have their best interests at heart.

The infamous Pygmalion in the Classroom study, where, unbeknownst to their teachers, the test scores of two incoming fourth-grade groups—one high-achieving, the other low—were reversed, provides a sobering empirical demonstration of the power a teacher's attitude toward his or her students can have over them. After a fairly brief interval with their new teachers, the children were tested again, and lo and behold, the former high achievers were suddenly performing at the level of the former low achievers and vice versa.

It is perhaps this very situation in the nation's schools, where our children are daily held hostage to the beliefs and expectations of a single adult—who increasingly remains a remote stranger in their lives—that has led people like Mary to start their own schools, or hundreds of thousands of homeschooling families to abandon the idea of school altogether. Whether at home, or in the wide array of alternative schools that now dot the nation, a vastly different model of teaching—including self-teaching—is at work.

It derives from a very different model of learning, one based on a fundamental respect for the centrality of the learner in the teaching/learning process. Such a shift of emphasis from teacher to learner in no way diminishes the value of good teaching and good teachers. There will always be a place in this world for people who can effectively teach others, whether those teachers wear some kind of professional badge or not. Frank, who calls himself a craftsman, not a teacher, was able to teach Jesse a set of valuable manual skills; at the same time, he helped Jesse do some important growing up.

The majority of practitioners in all of the varied alternatives to conventional schooling—homeschoolers very much included—operates according to a model of learning that, above all, honors the personhood of the learner. It reviles against coercion and respects the right of the learner to codetermine the conditions under which he or she will engage in the process. It holds volition and choice paramount. It maintains a bedrock faith in every child's inborn desire to learn and grow, to become knowledgeable, effective, and competent. And finally, it recognizes the validity of independent learning and self-teaching, where teacher and learner simply occupy the same being.

Recent brain/mind research is on the verge of confirming approaches to education that replace coercion with free choice, teacher-centeredness with child-centeredness, competition with cooperation, enforced togetherness with opportunities for solitary pursuits, management with autonomy, memorization with exploration and discovery, grading with self-assessment, and obligation with exuberance.

Joseph Chilton Pearce writes extensively about the emerging new biology and field theory–based model of learning and human intelligence in *Evolution's End*, a title he chose to convey his growing concern over humanity's failure, thus far, to utilize the immense potential of the mind. Pearce states that all human knowledge is, in fact, innate, and that what we call learning is actually a process whereby deeply embedded development unfolds from the inside out in response to the right cues from the environment.

Echoing Howard Gardiner, Pearce views each individual as a collection of potential intelligences, and translating them from mere potentiality into our personal experience of them is what some call child development, or others education. Further, writes Pearce: "Nature's agenda unfolds these intelligences for their development within us at a time appropriate to each." We can fail to nurture an intelligence by pushing it too soon, waiting too long, or ignoring it altogether. All the infant/child wants to do is what nature intended, which is to build up structures of knowledge; all that he or she needs to do that is a sufficiently stimulating environment, or in Pearce's words, "to be surrounded by mature, intelligent intellects, open to mind's possibilities and tempered by heart's wisdom, recognizing that to the human all may be possible."

If we look to the ongoing research into the abundant intelligence with which babies are born, this whole idea of innate knowing begins to sound a lot less mystical. For instance, we now know that a healthy newborn baby (who has not been excessively traumatized during the birth process) will respond immediately to the image of a human face if held at a distance of six to twelve inches—the distance between a mother's face and nursing breast—since this genetically encoded visual circuit has already been hardwired for just that purpose.

Next, the stimulus of the initial face recognition will trigger the ripening of the baby's entire visual apparatus, which will then become the key that begins unlocking myriad doors in the infant's rapidly expanding intellect. The very same is true for the development of language, whose building blocks are equally hardwired into a baby's neural circuitry and are only waiting for the appropriate environmental stimuli in order to begin gradually coalescing and unfolding into articulate speech.

Does this notion of "hardwired" intelligence negate the importance of teaching? Hardly, because it is nature's imperative, according to Pearce, that no human learning occur without a stimulus from an already mature form of that particular intelligence. The kind of stimulus he is referring to, however, is anything but mechanical or one-dimensional; rather it is holographic. Teachers influence students on a myriad of subtle—or not so subtle—levels, as the "Pygmalian" study so dramatically confirms. Here Pearce reminds us how it is estimated that 95 percent of all learning takes place below the level of conscious awareness, meaning that students in a teacher/student interaction are taking in far more than just information or the demonstration of a particular skill. They are also affected by teachers' moods, beliefs, and attitudes, as well as by how teachers feel about themselves, their students, and what they are teaching.

As Pearce says, "Teachers teach who they are"—meaning that beneath all of the trappings, teachers teach by modeling, not by instructing, managing, or evaluating student performance, the foundations of the role as it is typically practiced in conventional school settings. Therefore, teaching can no longer be viewed simply as a process whereby one person more skilled than another breaks down a subject or a procedure into small enough pieces for the student to digest successfully.

We urgently need a new vocabulary to describe the teaching/learning interface. The old Western scientific, cause-and-effect paradigm doesn't suffice anymore, since we have expanded our understanding of the teaching/learning process to the point where we know it isn't something that one person does to another, but rather is a form of interactive collaboration occurring on many different levels. Since the knowledge and skills we previously believed needed to be taught to the student are already there waiting to be awakened, we can no longer accept the old schooling premise that the teacher is the cause and the student is the effect of the learning process.

Thus, when Missy, Nancy, and Mary are teaching children in the Free School, they are conscious of the importance of being present with the fullness of themselves. Missy realizes she isn't just teaching the *doing*—the skills and techniques—of drawing, rather she is modeling *being* an artist and loving art. She knows she is also modeling herself, and so at any given moment there might occur levels of sharing between her and the students that outwardly might have little to do with the "subject" of art.

The same is true for Nancy when she is teaching reading. What she is really doing is modeling the beauty, power, joy, and ease of reading. She's showing the kids for whom reading might not come as easily that reading is a pleasure, not a struggle. She never tries to force anyone to go any faster than they are currently ready, willing, or able to go. And like Missy, she's always available with her full self.

Whenever Mary teaches, and she still does from time to time, what she is actually doing is leading kids on a personal quest to discover how to embrace the totality of themselves, no-holds-barred. That is the way she has always lived her own life and kids instinctively understand and respond to her example.

THE PROPOSITION THAT a true teacher is a fully holistic model and not merely a taskmaster or a classroom manager means it is impossible for teachers to lead their students any farther than they have already taken themselves. One simply cannot model something one hasn't already experienced oneself. This, then, leads to the imperative that all of us who consider ourselves teachers, especially good ones, not only make sure we are fluent with the material we are teaching, but that we also pay careful attention to our own emotional health, as well as other matters of personal growth and development—and that we continue to do this on an ongoing basis. Everyone working with children of any age must strive to be whole persons. And this doesn't just include teachers in schools. Parents are—and should always be—among their kids' most important teachers.

For this reason more than any other Mary suggested in the school's early days that we institute a weekly personal growth group. "Group," as we simply call it, began in 1974, and has met nearly every Wednesday evening ever since. Here is where we work on our own personal life-issues and problems as they arise, as well as where we are able to delve more deeply into the emotional and spiritual dimensions of our evolving selves.

It is also here that we resolve the interpersonal conflicts that inevitably result from working together so closely. The work we do individually and together in group is instrumental in helping us keep our minds and hearts open to the kids we are coming into such close contact with every day in school.

I have a friend named John Lawry, who teaches future teachers at Marymount College in Poughkeepsie, New York. He once wrote an article, which he has since expanded into book-length form, entitled "*Caritas* in the Classroom: The Opening of the American Student's Heart." In it he confirms my belief—one that Joseph Chilton Pearce would readily embrace—in the primacy of openheartedness in the teaching process.

Professor Lawry writes that it is peculiar to the West to bypass the emotional connection between student and teacher. The article sprang from a personal discovery that his own classroom was transformed as he began reversing this tradition. He found that when he stepped from behind his mask of professional composure and began revealing his own emotional life, and when he started asking his students how they were feeling about themselves and their lives, their engagement in the learning process increased dramatically. Here he was modeling for them how to engage their students in the many years to come.

Lawry also refers to a little-known study showing that students of teachers who measure high in qualities such as empathy, psychological integrity, and positive regard have significantly better standardized test scores than students of teachers who measure low in those areas. While test scores can be interpreted in myriad ways for as many reasons, shouldn't it be obvious that openhearted teachers engender openhearted students, who in turn become more effective learners?

I think so.

13

Community

*C*hild X is born to a woman and a man living in one of the
populous metropolitan belts on either coast of the United
States. Sometime during the first three months of life, its
mother returns to her full-time job, placing Child X in a certified
day care situation. The father, as it turns out, could not afford to
take any unpaid leave from his full-time job when his child was
born; consequently, he has yet to establish a strong bond with it,
though he is a proud father and loves the infant very much.

Economic pressures and frequent exhaustion slowly erode
our young family's resolve to engage in family activities together,
with television in a variety of forms gradually becoming the primary leisure activity. Child X's weekday schedule consists of being
dropped off at the day care site on its father's way to work at
around 8:00 A.M. and picked up by its mother on her return from
same at approximately 5:30 P.M. After eating dinner upon the
father's arrival at about 6:30, our young child has just enough
time to watch a show on the Disney Channel before its 8:00 P.M.
bedtime. Weekends feature occasional family outings, usually to
the nearby suburban shopping mall; and often include long sessions of television and video viewing. Their apartment complex
allows no pets, and lacking a secure yard, the mother is afraid to
allow her child out of doors unsupervised. Although both parents
had practiced their religion of birth as children, neither have the
energy or inclination to attend any place of worship now, especially with a young child in tow.

Particularly during the fall and winter months, Child X develops frequent ear infections, which result in visits to the family's HMO where the young child is usually seen by a different pediatrician each time who issues the child a prescription for an antibiotic, generally clearing up the problem in three to five days. The mother has no one to whom she can turn over a sick child, and her lost work time adds significantly to the family's financial woes.

Meanwhile, the parents' romantic beginnings quickly become a distant memory, and as marital strife mounts, each member of the couple turns to their only friends—a handful of coworkers—for advice and support. A second child is born at this point, easing the friction temporarily. Unfortunately, the added stress of caring for a new baby ultimately becomes the last straw and before it reaches the age of five, Child X's parents separate permanently, with divorce following a year later. Child X and its new sibling remain with the mother, spending every other weekend with their father, who continues to live in the area. Once or twice each year they visit with their two sets of grandparents, who both live in distant cities.

In the fall of its sixth year, Child X enters kindergarten in the local public school, where it shares a classroom and a single adult with twenty-eight other five-year-olds, and then attends an after-school program until the arrival of its mother at 5:30 P.M. Things go okay initially; but in first grade the child's teacher begins to notice midway through the year that Child X is beginning to have difficulty maintaining focus for the entire lesson. The teacher notes this development on the child's report card, but is prohibited from calling the parents in for a conference by a teachers' union bargaining policy during a protracted contract dispute with the school district. Toward the end of that year, Child X starts to exhibit signs of incipient asthma and concerns over school performance are quickly overridden by anxiety regarding the child's health.

THAT SHOULD BE enough of an intentionally simplistic portrayal of a stereotypical child's life in late-twentieth-century America for the sake of arguing it is the loss of community perhaps more than any other single factor that is responsible for the existential *angst* currently plaguing the children of this nation. It is my entirely nonstatistical belief that a conservative estimate of the percentage of our children who are at least partially described by the above scenario would be somewhere around 50 percent. This burgeoning group of unbonded post–baby boom young people, raised in the isolation of the nuclear family—with its ever increasing tendency toward splitting up—has given rise to what has been dubbed by social commentators as Generation X, an entire generation of young people known for its deep sense of alienation and for its lack of connection to past or future.

I surmise that one reason the term *community* has entered the realm of jargon is because of an instinctive hope that if we simply say the word enough, somehow we will conjure it back into being. Certainly, a sense of community is something that a great many of us hunger for and that almost everyone thinks is a good idea. And yet it is a social reality that has been driven to near extinction, just as the indigenous peoples of this land were little more than a hundred years ago—both by the same forces, human greed and economic manifest destiny.

Before I go any further, some definitions are in order, since much of the original meaning of "community" has become obscured. A good attempt at pinning down the essential meaning of this elusive notion comes from M. Scott Peck in his classic treatise on the subject, *The Different Drum*. Peck prefaces his definition by saying that community is one of those ephemeral phenomena, like electricity or love, that defies one-sentence definitions. He then goes on to try:

> If we are going to use the word meaningfully we must restrict it to a group of individuals who have learned how to communicate honestly with each other, whose relationships go deeper than their masks of composure, and who have developed some significant commitment to rejoice together, mourn together, and to delight in each other, making the other's condition our own.

Peck's own response to his growing perception that community is a dying tradition in the modern world was to begin traveling around the country giving weekend-long workshops in which participants struggle together as a group to reach the above-described state. According to Peck, communities can have any number of forms or sizes and can be either temporary or long-term in duration. They can be centered around a shared location, e.g. a neighborhood or a dormitory; around a shared goal, e.g. a political action group or volunteer organization; around a shared set of ideals, e.g. a religious group; or simply around the desire to learn about community, as in Peck's workshops.

And then there are the groups of people around the country who have actually chosen to organize themselves into intentional communities of one kind or another. Examples of this enduring phenomenon are not to be found only in the countercultural commune movement of the 1960s and 1970s. A number of so-called utopian communities were established at various points in the early history of America, and there are hundreds of different intentional communities in existence today. There is also the most recent crystallization of the human urge to live among others in a more shared fashion, known as "co-housing," where participants live conjointly and own their own homes privately, but cooperate in many shared functions such as land use and child care.

THE FREE SCHOOL is actually a community within a community within a community. Let me explain. First there is the school, which absolutely qualifies as a community using Peck's strict definition. Next, there is the Free School Community—I will use a capital "C" here hopefully to avoid confusion—which gradually coalesced in close conjunction with the school's organic development. These are the dozen or so families today who share with a great deal of intention a number of common concerns, enterprises, and tasks, including but not limited to the Free School itself. I described these in some detail in the opening chapter on the history of the school.

And finally there is the old, multiethnic neighborhood of which we are one distinct ingredient. I'm not sure the neighborhood as a whole would pass Peck's test, but it would come close in certain respects. It has somehow managed to hang on to its identity as a neighborhood in the classical sense of the term, having preserved the tradition of neighborliness and shared concern where neighbors look out for each other, even though they may not see eye to eye on matters of the larger world. Thus, while the neighborhood is not a community per se, most residents would say that they feel a sense of community, which is why they choose to live here, in spite of the problems any inner-city area is bound to have today.

A diagram of our situation here in Albany would look like three more or less concentric rings, with the school in the center and the neighborhood on the outside. Then you would have to draw all sorts of arrows pointing this way and that way because there is an almost constant interaction between the three circles. For example, Free School Community members serve on the board of directors of the neighborhood association from time to time, and frequently we are activists involved in issues of local concern. Neighborhood meetings were held in the Free School until they moved around the corner to an Italian restaurant whose delicious food is an excellent incentive to attend.

There is an ever present danger that dysfunctional, in group/out group dynamics will arise. This tends not to happen very often because everyone is always free to participate at whatever level they feel comfortable with. For instance, some Free School families are members of the Free School Community and the majority are not—we are careful not to proselytize the concept of community in any way, shape, or form. Some parents heavily involve themselves in the life of the school, and others not at all, and that is perfectly all right, too. We have always strictly avoided any policies of mandatory involvement, and longtime observers of our school tell me they have never detected any signs of a select inner circle. If ever someone does express feelings of being left out, we stop and try to resolve them.

Mary intended the school itself to be a real community from the outset. Even when it consisted of only Mary and her son, she held the Free School as a shared venture between "teacher" and "student." This founding principle remained in place as the new school began to grow dramatically in size. It is important to note here that Mary never thought the school should exist solely to meet the needs of the children, because she believed it was equally important for it to encompass the growth requirements of the adults as well.

Perhaps what makes the Free School a true community more than anything else is the fact that it is a place where everyone, students and teachers alike, brings his or her whole self—the good parts and the bad parts—each day, as well as all of the extensions of self that might be in play at any given time. For example, if one of the kids has gotten a new kitten, she'll bring the news (and sometimes the kitten) to school and we'll all rejoice with her; if someone is having a birthday, we'll celebrate it; if someone has suffered a loss, we will mourn with that person; if there's a serious illness at home, we'll pray together; and so on. If a child's parents have been fighting and he or she has come to school angry or frightened, or both, then those feelings are welcome, too. Or maybe Betsy and I are in the middle of a big argument. The school community will have compassion for us, and if we want, it will try to help us work whatever it is through so that we can check our troubles at the door. In other words, the Free School is a community because it is a place where everyone actively cares about everyone else.

But why, in the context of school—or any environment where kids come together specifically to learn—raise the flag of community up such a tall pole?

Not too long ago, a reporter from a local newspaper inadvertently provided me with the answer. He had just spent an entire day with us so that he could write a feature-length profile of the school. During a wrap-up chat in the afternoon, he shared a very astute observation, one that I'd never heard expressed quite in this way before. He began by noting how in most classrooms in most schools, there are always at least a couple of kids who are loners, who seem withdrawn, or "out of it" in some way. We found we could both vividly remember this phenomenon from our own childhoods spent in many such classrooms. The journalist then went on to say that he was quite taken by not having seen a single child in our school who fit this pattern, for which he admitted he had been watching carefully. All of the children in the Free School, he noted, appeared to be "in the flow." Everyone always seemed to be actively engaged in something, whether alone, in pairs, or in groups of various sizes.

He asked me why I thought this was so. My response—community.

For Scott Peck, community is the act of "making the other's condition our own." Mary, in a speech she gave at Carnegie Hall in 1991, defined it simply as "total mutual support." The reporter's definition, I think, would have been equally simple: When no one is ever left out. In any event, community, however defined, remains at the center of everything the Free School does. I was particularly pleased by the reporter's assessment because it was not coming, as it turned out, from a believer in freedom in the educational process. His lengthy story appeared with a number of critical and unfriendly asides, offering little to promote our image in the public eye. And yet still he managed to get the essence of who we are.

It cannot be stressed enough that notions of community should not be taken to mean some permanent state of blissful hunky-doriness. Things go wrong with regularity both in our school community and within the community of families in the middle ring of the above-mentioned diagram—the Community with the capital "C." Conflict is inevitable in the context of any community because there is such a high degree of intimacy involved. For this reason, Peck devotes an entire section of *The Different Drum* to what he terms "community maintenance." Here he states that in order for communities to stay active and healthy, it is imperative that they learn to "fight gracefully." This is precisely the purpose of the council meeting system in the school, and one that is mirrored in the Free School Community by the Wednesday evening group, which I described in the previous chapter. I might add that when there is a crisis brewing within the community, as happens now and again, we will sometimes hold "community council meetings," which are run just like council meetings in the school.

While we are careful to continue working at maintaining community well-being, we make sure not to allow our practice of community to develop into a solely inward-focused event or some sort of icon to pay homage to. We recognize the equal importance of reaching out. A fresh example would be our oldest class's recent trip to Puerto Rico to help the poor recover from severe hurricane damage. The project came about because several years ago Ruel Bernard, the father of two former Free School students, founded a grassroots organization whose mission is to work *with* families in a series of desperately impoverished squatters' villages on the island, helping them with the construction of homes, libraries, community centers, and safe water and septic systems. He named his not-for-profit "Building Community."

The class's very preparations for the trip were a demonstration of the power of community. Most of them were children of the working poor themselves, and yet in only two months they managed to raise more than five thousand dollars to cover the costs of the trip, including buying the materials needed to complete the septic system, which became their primary job while they were there. They raised the money by soliciting donations from relatives and local businesses, producing and selling an excellent literary magazine, and staging a seemingly endless series of raffles, dinners, and bake sales. This involved a great deal of hard work and the kids received a lot of support from the rest of the school community. Parents baked, teachers helped organize events, and a number of younger kids even eagerly helped to sell raffle tickets for them.

Then there was the week in Puerto Rico itself, where they were able to complete a very trying and unglamorous construction project under the relentless Caribbean sun. I wish Scott Peck could have been there to watch all the levels of community unfold. The kids worked right alongside the family they were aiding—who survive on a monthly welfare check of $112. Each day about half the group busied themselves with the not-so-small task of satisfying everyone's hunger and thirst. Manuela, the young mother of six, delighted in teaching our kids the finer points of native Puerto Rican cuisine, and every workday ended with a sumptuous peasant meal from which no one went away hungry. Julio and his two oldest sons formed a human cement-mixer, supplying Ruel and our kids with the mortar and concrete needed to build a proper septic tank and bathroom floor. Formerly the family would eliminate into a five-gallon plastic pail, which they then incinerated behind the "house," which was no more than a small, recycled plywood shack.

Meanwhile, on the first day when there was a lot of confusion as to just how to proceed with the project, along came a man from just down the squalid village's deeply rutted main "road." Juan, an unemployed construction worker who had built numerous such septic tanks under the flooded conditions Ruel, Julio, and the kids were facing, quickly appointed himself project manager and helped the group form a plan of attack. Before long Juan's wife and daughter, too, were a part of the rapidly growing, mud-covered family.

To keep our kids' spirits up, Julio's younger son got out the family's pony and started teaching Free Schoolers how to ride. Cross-lingual language instruction was ongoing, as our group spoke little Spanish and the family little English. And each exhausting workday ended with all of Julio's boys leading the tired, dirty Free School volunteers down to the river to bathe and cool off.

The closeness of this motley, multicultural group grew with each new day. There were always unexpected surprises, like when one of the Free School boys had an allergic reaction to an insect bite and was severely ill for several hours. Lots of group support and a homeopathic remedy brought him around. With an enormous push on the final day, there was just enough time to complete the project by the week's end. The kids' stay concluded with a huge feast of celebration and thanks. Everyone was changed—we were indeed "building community."

WITH GENERATION X serving as a canary in the coal mine, the effects of the deprivation of community on the nation's children are becoming more pronounced all the time. Childhood asthma is increasing exponentially. So is the teenage suicide rate, especially if you include deaths from automobile accidents, drug overdoses, and AIDS fatalities. And violent crimes are being committed by younger and younger children every day. It's no wonder. Day care centers and before- and after-school programs are proliferating, dramatically increasing the extent to which kids—like many of their grandparents and great-grandparents—are warehoused far away from the main streets of modern life. Parents are more and more preoccupied with matters of economic survival, leaving less and less time and energy for bonding with their children. The family itself is under siege, as the extended family has already given way to the nuclear family, which is fast turning into an isolated mass of single-parent households.

We, the human family, have a problem. The kind of human disconnection I attempted to portray in the fictional opening vignette is proliferating in ways and at rates that cannot be measured. I once heard Dr. Michel Odent, an obstetrician-turned-midwife and one of the leaders of the international natural-childbirth movement, express his deep concern in this way: "It is no accident that the nuclear family and the nuclear age coincided historically." Odent's life's work is about saving the mother- and father-infant bond from extinction so that humanity will not lose the wherewithal to come together to solve the problems threatening us as a species.

In case you were beginning to wonder, I'm not going to hold out some glorified notion of community as the solution to the world's problems, although, admittedly, it's tempting. If one deeply identifies with certain ideas, as I do with community and freedom in education; and if one is a problem-solver by nature, as I also am, then there is always the urge to feel, Wait, I have the answer! If everyone just lived in small, intentional communities and started up free schools, everything would be fine. But this is absurd. Even simple problems have multiple causes and multiple solutions.

Nevertheless, I do believe that if we are to survive the current set of dilemmas we have created for ourselves and enable our children to move into a more certain future, we must find ways, however small, to restore forms of community to modern life.

I'm reminded of the activist's slogan: Think Globally, Act Locally. Thinking globally, and returning to the subject at hand—children and learning—it seems to me that one major source of the trouble is the extent to which our corporate economy has succeeded in turning children, as well as their education, into commodities. On weekdays we store kids in large warehouses to keep them out of sight and out of mind, so that they will neither compete for nor in any way impede economic activity in the marketplace. While they are in those warehouses, we condition them to become obedient, passive consumers, insuring that upon their release as "adults" they will become virtual slaves to that very same marketplace.

We have removed children from the picture entirely. Take a walk through the downtown business district of any city on any working day if you don't believe me. That's why, whenever I go to the bank or the post office, I invite kids from school to accompany me. So often the adults we encounter these days don't quite know what to make of them; they stare at the kids as though they were aliens from outer space.

IVAN ILLICH ONCE argued that "deschooling" society would be the best way to reconnect children to the web of community life. He was not calling for the society to eliminate schools as such, but to eliminate the monopoly schools have on children's time, energy, and location. Do that, claimed Illich, and children will of necessity start finding their way back toward the heart of their villages, towns, and urban centers, confronting the adults directly with the necessity of creating ways to reinclude the next generation of citizens.

Even in the 1960s, Illich was branded an iconoclast and a dreamer, so one can only imagine what his reception would be like today. And yet countless homeschooling families are currently doing exactly as he suggested. They are taking their children out of storage (or they aren't putting them there in the first place) and are busy reintegrating them into the life of the family. Then, as they mature, they are inventing an assortment of ways of gaining them access to the adult working world via networks of internships and apprenticeships, and small family-run businesses and cottage industries.

Homeschoolers are also creating their own forms of community by coming together to foster a variety of cooperative learning/playing opportunities for their kids. The movement is growing fast, as more and more parents discover that they don't have to cede control of their children's hearts, minds, and spirits to the society's system of compulsory education. What if the entire nation elected to follow their example?

I cite the efforts of homeschoolers not to wave the flag of homeschooling as *the* answer, but to use them as one good example of local action. And I see other encouraging signs of change. The number of small, independent schools—of a dozen different types and philosophies—seems to have taken a sudden jump. Some more than others function as communities in the purer sense of the word, but taken as a whole, their very diversity helps to preserve an important dimension of community. Contrary to popular logic, like-mindedness and community make lousy dance partners.

There is also a continuing proliferation of public educational alternatives, led by individuals determined to take advantage of already existing public funding and still break free of the lockstep schooling mentality based on regimentation and compulsion. I remain deeply cynical about the possibility of anyone ever fundamentally reforming public education—the concept simply occupied too much false ground from the outset—but I salute any and all efforts to improve the lot of the young people housed therein. These days many of the secondary-level alternatives are introducing initiatives like mentorship, apprenticeship programs, and community service work, which actively involve them in the world of today.

And more and more there seems to be a growing awareness among parents of the need to become more involved in the education of their children. More parents are demanding an active involvement in school policy making. They are unlocking the doors and opening the windows of the public schools and insisting that there be greater levels of exchange between school and outside world. For better *and* for worse, "community" seems to be on the tip of everybody's tongue these days.

MY PERSONAL WINDOW on the world is that of having spent the past twenty-five years as a teacher, parent, and citizen, immersed in the ongoing practice of community and of discovering new ways of enabling children to grow into autonomous, fully developed adult beings. Such a perspective, grounded as it is in the imperfect world of human experience, leaves me hopeful and cynical all in the same breath.

It remains my profound belief, based on such experience, that children profit immensely from the exposure to community that they receive in our school—perhaps today more than ever. It establishes an interior template that will help guide them toward a future filled with personal meaning based on their ability to connect meaningfully with others. Otherwise, without any solid sense of belonging, they may drift about unanchored. This makes them easy marks for an economy dependent upon a steady influx of alienated half-people ready to substitute the consumption of material goods for the pleasure and fulfillment located in the bonds of family, friendship, and shared endeavor.

Toward this end, I put forth the Free School as one possible model of school as community. Again, is it *the* answer? Of course not. I am ever heedful of Illich's warning that systematized, compulsory schooling represents an implicit structural obstacle to the existence of real human community—and the Free School does its level best to avoid that pitfall. Our kids come to school because they want to, and we continually encourage and facilitate their interaction with the world around them.

Meanwhile, there are a thousand and one ways to create community, just as there are a thousand and one ways for children to learn to read, write, and figure. The important thing to remember here is that community, more than anything else, is a state of mind. It doesn't require special equipment, training, or staffing. What it does take is people's willingness to overcome their resistance to coming together, and then to hanging in together, until they can fulfill their common purpose.

Conclusion

*T*he Free School's story doesn't end here, but I trust I've told enough of it to portray at least some of the beauty and the practicality of operating a school according to the principles of freedom, community, and trust in every child's inborn drive to learn and grow.

With the arrival of second-generation students and teachers, it appears that the Free School will be around for years to come. Three former students have come back to teach thus far, every one a special blessing. None, as yet, have decided to make a career of it. But each, not surprisingly, has proven to be a natural and gifted teacher. We hope both that they will return one day and that more will follow in their footsteps. Somehow I expect this will be the case.

We will go on modeling real community-based education for an increasingly atomized nation. The reason we do this, as Jung once wrote, is that human beings can only fully "individuate" in the context of a larger community. It's a grand paradox, and by it he meant that none of us can reach our full, individual potential alone in a cave or off on some sacred mountaintop. It takes the constant give and take, and push and pull, between individual and community to bring us into full ownership of all of the unique gifts granted each of us at birth.

We will also continue providing safe haven to a handful of local children each year who are in danger of falling victim to the dark shadow of our compulsory education system. We won't win them all, and we won't save the world this way—or will we?

Hasn't it been said that if you truly save one child, then you *have* saved the world? Eat your words while you rest in peace, dear old A. S. Neill; I know you would be pleased that Mary has shown many times over how children of the underclass can benefit from the freedom to chart their own course.

And we will keep fostering the growth of other children who would probably fare well in most any setting, but who choose to learn in an environment where their individuality and autonomy are respected and encouraged. We will keep demonstrating that living and learning are synonyms, as are freedom and respect. And we will keep learning from our kids, for whom static concepts like "education" have very little meaning.

We are receiving an ever increasing number of phone calls, letters, and visits from people everywhere who are interested in learning about genuine alternatives to the standard version of school, despite the waves of conservatism currently washing over American society. Thus it appears we are answering a growing need for information and inspiration regarding different ways of going about teaching and learning—and living—that work. Old 1960s free schools like ours—there are still a few dozen around—aren't anachronisms, and we aren't messiahs of some glorified new age, either. But we do bear an important message, one based on decades of hard-earned experience—and one that many still find hard to embrace: Children learn best when they do so for their own reasons, when they are respected as intelligent, responsible beings, and when they are free to move about and question within living, loving, exciting environments that are not sealed off from the outside world.

Do these principles require the pattern of organization called "school"? Absolutely not. Schools, as Illich, later Holt, and still later Gatto have all gone to great lengths to point out, nearly always have—and always will—set themselves up in opposition to most or all of them. While some schools do a better job than others of avoiding what Illich calls "the corrosive effects of compulsory schooling," the fact remains that generations of state-enforced, centrally managed education have quite literally schooled our modern minds, both individual and collective, out of the wherewithal to picture things any other way.

In other words, the current generation of parents is almost entirely dependent on the notion of schooling as it now exists, having so thoroughly internalized its myths: that education is a scarce commodity of which a prescribed amount must "be gotten" before a person can become a competent adult, that children learn only in the company of professionally trained and licensed teachers, and that the system of public education in this country is a democratic institution, which, with only a little more tinkering, will one day soon begin delivering life, liberty, and the pursuit of happiness equally to all of the nation's children.

In order to expose these myths for what they are, we need to keep discovering new ways—and rediscovering old ones—that will enable us to turn back the rising tide of dependency and artificiality in modern life. We need to keep increasing our awareness of the gap between ourselves and the true sources of learning, sustenance, and meaning in our own and our children's lives—while our consumption-driven economy stops at nothing to lure us away from them.

Revisiting Illich one final time, if the opportunities for learning outside of school were once again abundant, there would be no need for "education" as such. While notions of a return to a romanticized past are just that— romantic notions—we can and must keep shooting the gaps in the armor of the modern-day marketplace, going beyond tokens like "national bring- your-child-to-work day." We must continue struggling to readmit our children to the main current of American culture, not by worshiping them or handing them privileges on a silver platter; but first by including them and then by insisting that they earn their positions of responsibility and respect. When kids know an opportunity to gain valuable life experience is for real, they almost always respond in kind.

At the same time, let us not ignore the fact that these are largely white, middle-class ideas. As Jonathan Kozol so starkly depicted in his latest book, *Amazing Grace*, we remain two separate nations, one white and one not white, and the glimpses of hope in the increasingly segregated ghettos of our major cities are few and far between.

There are no momentous conclusions to be had regarding the subject at hand. No matter how much we reevaluate and reformulate our approaches to education, on all levels—sociological, intellectual, emotional, and spiritual—education as a social institution will never, in and of itself, solve any of the world's problems.

There simply are no one-dimensional answers or universal formulas. The world has always been filled with injustice and paradox and confusion and danger, just as it has with compassion and truth and faith and courage. What sustains humanity is a miracle of hope: within every child there exists a hardy seed of wonder and exuberance.

It is one we must never fail to nurture and protect. And that is why, here in the Free School, we will keep on making it up as we go along.